CONSUMPTION IN CHINA ——

China Today series

CONSUMPTION IN CHINA

HOW CHINA'S NEW CONSUMER IDEOLOGY IS SHAPING THE NATION

LiAnne Yu

polity

The right of LiAnne Yu to be identified as Author of this Work has been asserted in accordance with the UK Copyright, Designs and Patents Act 1988.

First published in 2014 by Polity Press

Polity Press
65 Bridge Street
Cambridge CB2 1UR, UK

Polity Press
350 Main Street
Malden, MA 02148, USA

ISBN-13: 978-0-7456-6970-0 (hardback)
ISBN-13: 978-0-7456-6971-7 (paperback)

A catalogue record for this book is available from the British Library.

Typeset in 11.5 on 15 pt Adobe Jenson Pro
by Toppan Best-set Premedia Limited
Printed and bound in Great Britain by Clays Ltd, St Ives PLC

The publisher has used its best endeavours to ensure that the URLs for external websites referred to in this book are correct and active at the time of going to press. However, the publisher has no responsibility for the websites and can make no guarantee that a site will remain live or that the content is or will remain appropriate.

Every effort has been made to trace all copyright holders, but if any have been inadvertently overlooked the publisher will be pleased to include any necessary credits in any subsequent reprint or edition.

For further information on Polity, visit our website: www.politybooks.com

Contents

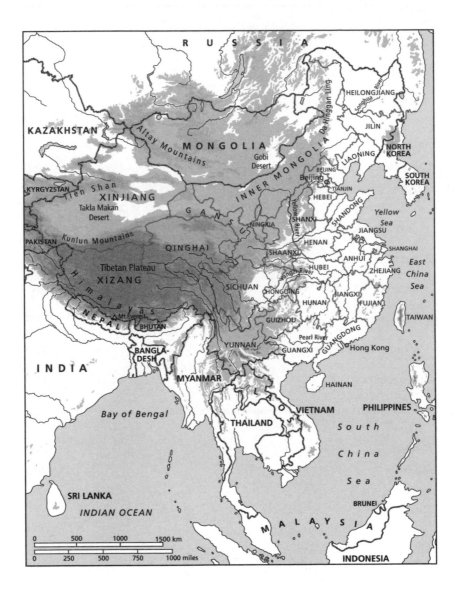

Chronology

1894–5	First Sino-Japanese War
1911	Fall of the Qing dynasty
1912	Republic of China established under Sun Yat-sen
1927	Split between Nationalists (KMT) and Communists (CCP); civil war begins
1934–5	CCP under Mao Zedong evades KMT in Long March
December 1937	Nanjing Massacre
1937–45	Second Sino-Japanese War
1945–9	Civil war between KMT and CCP resumes
October 1949	KMT retreats to Taiwan; Mao founds People's Republic of China (PRC)
1950–3	Korean War
1953–7	First Five-Year Plan; PRC adopts Soviet-style economic planning
1954	First constitution of the PRC and first meeting of the National People's Congress
1956–7	Hundred Flowers Movement, a brief period of open political debate
1957	Anti-Rightist Movement
1958–60	Great Leap Forward, an effort to transform China through rapid industrialization and collectivization

March 1959	Tibetan Uprising in Lhasa; Dalai Lama flees to India
1959–61	Three Hard Years, widespread famine with tens of millions of deaths
1960	Sino–Soviet split
1962	Sino–Indian War
October 1964	First PRC atomic bomb detonation
1966–76	Great Proletarian Cultural Revolution; Mao reasserts power
February 1972	President Richard Nixon visits China; "Shanghai Communiqué" pledges to normalize US–China relations
September 1976	Death of Mao Zedong
October 1976	Ultra-Leftist Gang of Four arrested and sentenced
December 1978	Deng Xiaoping assumes power; launches Four Modernizations and economic reforms
1978	One-child family planning policy introduced
1979	USA and China establish formal diplomatic ties; Deng Xiaoping visits Washington
1979	PRC invades Vietnam
1982	Census reports PRC population at more than one billion
December 1984	Margaret Thatcher co-signs Sino-British Joint Declaration agreeing to return Hong Kong to China in 1997
1989	Tiananmen Square protests culminate in June 4 military crackdown
1992	Deng Xiaoping's Southern Inspection Tour re-energizes economic reforms
1993–2002	Jiang Zemin is president of PRC, continues economic growth agenda

November 2001	WTO accepts China as member
August 2002	World Summit on Sustainable Development held in Johannesburg; PRC ratifies 1997 Kyoto Protocol to the United Nations Framework Convention on Climate Change
2003–13	Hu Jintao is president of PRC
2002–3	SARS outbreak concentrated in PRC and Hong Kong
2006	PRC supplants USA as largest CO_2 emitter
August 2008	Summer Olympic Games in Beijing
2010	Shanghai World Exposition
2012	Xi Jinping appointed General-Secretary of the CCP (and President of PRC from 2013)

Acknowledgments

First and foremost, I would like to thank the editors of Polity Press. Jonathan Skerrett showed just the right combination of encouragement, inspiration, and whip-cracking attention to deadlines. Emma Longstaff somehow found me, and I thank her from the bottom of my heart for giving me the chance to do this and convincing me this would be an extraordinary adventure. And it has been.

I am fortunate to know so many people who live in China, study China, write about China, or otherwise obsess over Chinese media, food, technology, fashion, gender issues, and youth culture. Whether they come from academic or professional backgrounds, or are (in at least one case) avid food bloggers driving around China in a motor home, they have taught me so much. Special thanks to Elaine Ann, Susan Darwin, Donna Flynn, Karl Gerth, Michael Griffiths, Amy Hanson, Chris Liu, Kelvin Ma, Daniel Makoski, Dara McCaba, Didier Perrot-Minot, Fiona Reilly, Michael McCune, Patricia Pao, Renee Hartmann, Michael Stanant, and Mag Wong. I am also fortunate to be part of an extraordinary writing community, which helped me to remember to write from a place of authenticity. Special thanks to Chris DeLorenzo of Laguna Writers, and my Puerto Vallarta and Thursday night writing comrades.

The people who deserve the most credit for this book are the hundreds of people in China whom I have met over the last decade, spent time with, and persuaded to be my research "subjects." They are always amazed that I find their lives so interesting. "This is just normal behavior – everybody does it. I'm not special," one young man said to me once when I asked why he spent such a large proportion of his meager income on luxury brands. For me, what is extraordinary is exactly that – how "normal" it has become in China to associate consumption with aspiration. One young woman, whom we will meet in this book, described her love of a particular auto brand in this way: "For me, the Jeep Wrangler represents freedom and passion. That is what I am pursuing in my life. I will drive it to the mountains, to the grassland, and to the desert. My Jeep will drive me to freedom." This book is dedicated to all the people in China who have been so generous with their time in telling me their stories and helping me see the world through their eyes.

1   Introduction

The first time I went shopping in China, I got yelled at and ignored. The year was 1990, and I was on a year-long foreign-exchange program at Beijing University, along with a group of a dozen other University of California students. We had studied Mandarin fervently, trying to perfect our Beijing accents. In our sociology and political science classes we had studied the transition from Communism under Mao Zedong to a free-market economy under Deng Xiaoping. And, just the year before, we had anxiously followed the news about the democracy movement and subsequent June 4th military crackdown on Tiananmen Square. But no one in our cohort had ever been to China, and the images that confronted us seemed contradictory. On the one hand, the city streets were packed with thousands of bicycle riders wearing unisex blue uniforms, a homogenous mass of working-class people. On the other hand, we were told that China was the new frontier for global multi-national companies. The country seemed to be in between worlds, still largely socialist in nature but with market reform taking root here and there.

Back in 1990, the shopping experience, however, still reflected what China had been, rather than where it would be in the next two decades. So, on that fateful first experience of shopping in a state-run store near campus, I asked in my politest Mandarin if the shopkeeper could show me some of the hot-water thermoses on the shelf behind the counter. Products in state-run stores were not kept out in the open where shoppers could browse on their own. The shopkeeper controlled access to everything. Alas, this shopkeeper felt that her newspaper was more important than me, her customer. I was left wondering if my Chinese classes had somehow failed me. At my fifth attempt to ask her if I could please see the water thermos, she suddenly snapped, uttered an expletive, and finally pulled the item off the shelf for me. After inspecting it I noticed that the lid did not screw on properly, and tried to ask her for another one. That was just too much for her. She scowled, put the thermos back on the shelf, turned up her radio, and simply ignored me. I never got my water thermos that day, and walked back to my dorm bewildered by that experience. It was my introduction to the surly service that was not uncommon in China's state-run stores, in which employment was guaranteed and shopkeepers had no incentive to please their customers or employers. An activity I had thoroughly taken for granted – shopping – had become something I had to learn how to do under a new set of circumstances.

In addition to the surly service, the state-run stores displayed little variety in goods. Snickers bars and Pringles chips, a staple for many of us young Americans, were hard to come by, except in specialty stores catering to foreigners. There were only a few TV stations available at that time – all of them state-run – featuring propaganda-laden programming. The wide boulevards of Beijing were lined with Communist party slogans and not the advertising billboards we were used to seeing back home. There were no malls or supermarkets, and no international chains such as McDonald's. For most everyday life products, there was little choice between brands or quality. Toilet paper came in one variety – rough and vivid pink.

There were options, but only for those with money, connections or foreign passports. The Friendship Store was state run, stocking imported items from the West, such as chocolate bars, peanut butter, and the otherwise forbidden copies of magazines such as *Time*. It only accepted foreign exchange as currency, and as such, was a tightly controlled space, not the kind of place where Chinese families could wander into freely. Luxury hotels had started to appear in the city as well. The New World Hotel featured one of the city's first authentic Italian restaurants (complete with a Filipino guitar player), a bowling alley, and a small market stocking canned foreign foods and imported toothpaste. Like the Friendship Store, the hotels were heavily guarded, and did not welcome the general Chinese public. Their customers were primarily Westerners, Japanese, and overseas Chinese.

In 1990, Beijing was not yet the cosmopolitan hub it would become in the two decades to follow. We foreign-exchange students elicited looks of wonder among the locals. Even those among us who were Chinese-American and could speak Mandarin fluently were easily identified as foreign through our dress, hairstyles, and larger builds. On buses, people stared at us in our Nike shoes, Levi jeans, and Gap t-shirts. It was not hard to become acutely aware of the economic disparities between us and our Chinese peers. This was most obvious in our daily living standards. We had access to hot water showers every evening in our dorms, while the Chinese students were only allowed access to the bathhouse once a week. We ate the good white rice in the foreign-exchange students' cafeteria, whereas the Chinese student cafeterias served rough, gray rice, sometimes containing small pebbles. We thought nothing of buying bottles of Coke with our lunch, while such expenditures were considered extravagant by our local friends. But what differentiated our circumstances was not just our relative wealth, but also our mobility. We were free to travel outside our country, so long as we (or rather, our parents) could pay for it. For the Chinese students, foreign travel was a very distant dream. Not only were their income levels too low, but the Chinese state tightly regulated travel visas. This first experience in China, and the view from the inside that my kind and generous Chinese friends gave me, made me realize how much I had taken for granted as a middle-class American with endless consumer choices.

We did not realize it then, but 1990 was a watershed year in China. Deng Xiaoping instituted changes that would hasten economic development, transforming the lifestyles of the country's residents – especially those well positioned in the biggest coastal cities of Shanghai, Beijing, and Guangzhou. In just three decades after Deng proclaimed that "to get rich is glorious," China has gone from being one of the most isolated and poorest nations to the world's second largest economy, second only to the USA. This economic boom has two, interrelated facets. One is China's rise as a site of production for multi-national corporations taking advantage of the country's abundant labor in order to churn out competitive products that line retail shelves all around the world. The second is the increased spending power of Chinese nationals themselves, who consume an ever burgeoning array of goods and services.

A few statistics will demonstrate how far the country has come in just the last few decades:

+ There are now over one million millionaires in China.
+ China has taken over the USA as the largest car market in the world.
+ In 2012, China overtook the US to become the world's largest market for luxury goods.
+ The number of internet users in China has exceeded 457 million, nearly one and a half times the total US population. The number of mobile phone users hit one billion in 2012.
+ Chinese tourists spent more on shopping while traveling in 2010 than tourists from any other nation in the world. Thirty percent of Burberry's sales in London are to Chinese tourists.
+ China now has the largest number of home buyers every year.

(China Luxury Network, retrieved January 20, 2013)

One of the most reliable indicators of China's economic emergence is the intense interest that corporations have in selling their products in China. Market research as a field is booming in China, as foreign executives and marketers turn to experts on China's consumer habits to understand how they can expand their businesses. A sign that corporations take the Chinese market very seriously is the fact that instead of merely shipping their already successful products to China, they are also creating locally appropriate offerings. For example, KFC, the first Western fast-food restaurant to open in China, offers rice porridge with preserved egg along with its standard fried-chicken dishes. BMW, recognizing that China is now the world's biggest market for new cars, has developed sedans that suit Chinese consumer preferences. This means bigger back seats, where owners spend their in-car time, as employing chauffeurs is a common practice among the affluent. Haagen Dazs sells mooncakes alongside its premium ice-cream. Levi Strauss introduced a brand called Denizen in Shanghai, designed to fit Chinese body types. A trip down the yogurt aisle at WalMart reveals varieties made with such Chinese flavors as red bean, aloe, lychee, and even gelatinized donkey skin. In stark contrast to the dearth of products available in state-run shopping malls as recently as the early 1990s, today consumers can choose from a bewildering array of goods localized for their tastes.

OVERVIEW OF THE BOOK

This book explores the transformation of consumer experiences in China over the last two decades. Shoddy state-run stores have made way for modern, gargantuan malls featuring European, Japanese, and American luxury brands. Blue and gray uniforms have made way for global fashion brands. Even Communist leaders have abandoned the image of a simple, peasant lifestyle for European cars, French wines, and American-style suburban homes. China's new rich are attracting the attention of the world's companies, who vie for market dominance in everything from soft drinks to smartphones. Today, messages to consume more stem from everywhere. Advertisements are as relentless and ubiquitous as socialist propaganda posters once were in China's public spaces. Even the Chinese state encourages its citizens to spend more on vacations, cars, homes, and raising children, as a way to stimulate its economy. Chinese consumers are, in ever greater numbers, buying luxury goods, traveling abroad, and even celebrating the very un-Communist holiday of Christmas by shopping. When I visit Beijing's shiny shopping centers today, I cannot believe that my experience with the surly retail worker in the state-run store took place just twenty years ago.

However, while such changes are often discussed in celebratory tones, especially in business literature, consumer culture in China has produced a mix of consequences. The increased ability to buy things and the ever burgeoning variety of goods available have led to environmental degradation, corrupt practices, and food-safety issues. Areas of life that were once free of market influences, such as childhood education, housing, and gender identities, are now becoming thoroughly and relentlessly commodified (Schor and Holt 2000). Furthermore, after several decades of living under a strict socialist ideology in which wealth and signs of class difference were stamped out, inequality has come back with a vengeance, as the difference between the wealthy and the poor becomes exacerbated each year.

Consumer culture is thus complex and messy, providing delight, community, and freedom, as well as stress, competition, and the pressure of keeping up. This mixed dynamic is not unique to China. However, because of the scale of changes to China's economic, social, and technological structures that have occurred in an extraordinarily short period of time, we can observe radical transformations in people's everyday lives within just a generation or even half a generation. The compressed nature of China's consumer revolution, as well as the contextually unique circumstances of such changes, lead to consumer behaviors and expectations that do not necessarily follow the patterns of other developed markets. Whether Chinese consumers will develop "just like" consumers elsewhere in the world on some common evolutionary path is still to be seen, but in this book I explore how consumer patterns in China both validate and challenge established consumption theories.

This book is based on the observations and ethnographic research I conducted in China over a twenty-year period. I first lived in China as a foreign-exchange student in 1990, and after that returned regularly to conduct consumer research on behalf of global companies seeking to understand the market. Because of my own hybrid background as a PhD anthropologist working as a consumer insights strategist for Fortune 500 companies, I borrow inspiration from both the academic and business worlds. From academia, I borrow frameworks around the commodification of goods, identity formation, and social distinction. From business thinkers, I borrow frameworks focused on consumer aspirations and the symbolic values of brands and products. In addition to ethnographic research with Chinese consumers, this book also reflects my conversations with consumer insights experts. They include academics, advertising professionals, and bloggers living and traveling across China (in one case, in a motor home). My goal was to base this book on a variety of perspectives, from the consumers themselves to outsiders with a range from analytical to personal views.

This book is not based on a large quantitative sample, with the aim of presenting definitive facts backed by statistically sound figures. Rather, it is based on qualitative research and deep dives into the lives of several dozen individuals with whom I have spent time over the years. This book highlights common threads and experiences around what people are consuming, why they make these choices, and what this says about who they are today and who they aspire to be in the future. As we shall see in this book, these stories and vignettes from their lives illuminate what it feels like and what it means to be a consumer in China today.

As it is elsewhere in the world, the topic of consumption in China is vast. Everyone consumes, from the newly minted billionaires to the rural poor. This book is limited primarily to China's first-tier cities, and within that, the bulk of the focus is on Beijing and Shanghai, where I have spent the most time and conducted the most research. This is certainly not by accident. The focus of my corporate clients has, for the last decade, been primarily on China's biggest, most cosmopolitan cities, where income levels are at the highest, and the numbers of middle and upper-class consumers are the largest. In other words, the primary focus of this book is on people who live comfortably and do not have to worry about meeting their basic needs around food, clothing, and shelter. They are consumers who have immediate access to whatever they may desire through myriad shopping centers as well as the world of e-commerce. At the same time, this book does not focus on the economic elite – China's millionaires and billionaires, who live extraordinary lives by any country's standards. Rather, the study is based on China's emerging middle and upper middle-class consumers. We will explore what this means in greater detail later on, but for now, I borrow a definition from Michael McCune, Director at Iconoculture, who defines the middle class as those who still need to make some tradeoffs between what they desire and what they can afford. What I appreciate about this deceptively simple definition is the focus on "tradeoffs," which allows us to explore consumer constraints as well as opportunities.

My focus on urban, well-off consumers is not meant as an argument that they are the most important people to study when it comes to consumption in China. From a business perspective, China's base of the pyramid consumers represent a huge opportunity, as corporations vie to create the laptops, mobile phones, laundry detergents, and household goods that meet their functional and emotional needs as well as financial constraints. From an academic view, China cannot be truly understood holistically without exploring the lifestyles of the nearly 50 percent of the population that lives in rural areas, typically in conditions that have not changed much in fifty years. From a social justice perspective, China's economic "miracle story" must be tempered by the experiences of millions of migrants, urban poor, and working class who struggle to make ends meet as the state withdraws more of its social welfare programs.

Given the admittedly limited scope of this book, what I wish to do is bring to life the experiences of China's most "obvious" consumers — the ones that corporations covet and the Chinese state celebrates as a symbol of the country's prosperity. The period of time that my research encompasses — the early 1990s to 2013 — captures the perspectives of two distinct generations, representing very different consumer experiences. People who grew up under the most austere years of socialism are still alive, parenting and grandparenting, while their children, who have only known a prospering, capitalistic China, are coming of age, entering the workforce, and becoming fully fledged consumers themselves. Memories of life during the Cultural Revolution, when all signs of a bourgeois lifestyle were often violently stamped out, stand in contrast with the consumerist lifestyles of the present. This contrast is central to the exploration of this book. The consumer revolution today did not develop out of a vacuum, but rather in response to as well as in tension with the austere lifestyles of the very recent past. I have found that people in China, whether or not they are old enough to remember pre-reform lifestyles, are keenly aware of the fact that they are living in a remarkable period. By focusing on people's perceptions of change over the last few decades, and not just on the present, this book seeks to capture that awareness of transformation.

THE TRANSFORMATION FROM SOCIALISM TO CONSUMERISM

In order to understand the context within which China's current consumer culture has developed, let us briefly review China's recent history. By the early twentieth century, China had experienced the overthrow of its emperor by a nationalist government under Chiang Kai Shek, extreme pressure from the West to open up its markets, internal strife between regional warlords, and Japanese occupation during the Second World War. Mao Zedong, leader of the Chinese Communist Party, promised a restoration of China's dignity, self-reliance, and an end to the foreign imperialism that had ravaged the country. In 1949, the CCP defeated Chiang Kai Shek and established the People's Republic of China.

Once in power, the CCP developed a redistribution system based on a planned, top-down economy. Privately owned homes, businesses, and assets were seized. People's communes were established in the countryside, organizing peasants into large agricultural units. In urban areas, the CCP instituted the work-unit system, called the *danwei*, based on economic units such as factories and hospitals. Everyone belonged to a commune or *danwei*, which not only assigned and organized work duties but also provided for housing, meals, health care, education, and child care.

Most forms of free-market enterprises were banned by 1958. One's workplace thus determined people's standards of living. They allocated apartments, provided for social welfare, but also provided for most of the consumer items that had once been discretionary expenditures, such as entertainment and holiday treats. The state eliminated privately owned stores, restaurants, and entertainment centers. State-run stores provided people with basic necessities, which were distributed via a coupon system. The products in these stores, however, were limited, due to the country's increasingly isolationist policies in terms of global trade, and were thus in high demand despite their sometimes shoddy production. Life, for the average person, was characterized by standing in line, rationing, and scarcity (Naughton 1995). Those working in the stores were, like everyone else, assigned to their roles via their *danwei*, and had little incentive to serve their customers well (Otis 2012: 42).

What limited consumption options were available were subject to the critique and censure of not only the state but one's peers and family members. Such anti-bourgeois sentiment reached a high during the decade known as the Cultural Revolution, which lasted from 1966 to Mao's death in 1976. Mao called on China's youth to help him wage a violent class struggle against what he called the bourgeois elements, including his own enemies within the party. The youth organized themselves into Red Guard groups, persecuting anybody suspected of having a counter-revolutionary mindset or way of life. This included teachers, artists, writers, intellectuals, professionals such as doctors, or anyone who dared to speak out against Mao's extremism. Suspects were publicly humiliated, imprisoned, and tortured.

Throughout Mao's regime, the life of ordinary citizens revolved primarily around displaying the correct political ideology. Consumption practices became politicized and subject to public censure. Mao held up the unadorned, modest peasant lifestyle as the model for everyone on the path towards realizing a classless society. Women were called upon to exert their equality by cutting their hair, ridding themselves of make-up, high heels, and skirts, and dressing the same way as men. Foreign influences in art and literature were banned, replaced by Communist propaganda-driven operas, paintings, and books. For a time, the only text being studied in school was Mao's *Little Red Book*. Displaying any so-called bourgeois desires through dress, home décor, actions, or words could land one a stint in the rural re-education camps.

Mao's death in 1976 ushered in a sea change in the party's leadership and focus. By 1978, reformist Deng Xiaoping was solidly in control of the party, effectively reversing most of Mao's policies, which had devastated the nation's economy and agricultural industry. The new leadership reversed Mao's focus on heavy industry, and instead prioritized light industry, agriculture, and consumer products. A year later, the United States officially recognized the PRC, opening the doors to

American investment. Global companies took advantage of the cheap and abundant labor, moving their factories to China to produce low-cost goods. Made in China became a ubiquitous tag on items from toys to clothing to kitchen appliances. In 1992, Deng embarked on his famous tour of several economically forward cities, including Guangzhou, Shenzhen, Zhuhai, and Shanghai. During this tour, he spoke fervently about economic reform, garnering immense local support for his reformist platform. This trip is now seen as a watershed moment in the development of Shanghai and the south as the country's economic hubs.

Throughout the 1980s and 1990s, the communal systems were gradually dismantled as peasants were given more freedom to work the land and sell their products on the nascent but growing free market. Entrepreneurs began to set up shop and state-owned factories were transformed into privately owned businesses. Peddlers, street vendors, and small-scale private merchants began to reappear throughout the country. Joint ventures between the state and international retailers began to offer Chinese consumers options beyond the shoddily made domestic and Eastern European products that had characterized Mao's isolationist policies. By the early twenty-first century, massive glass and chrome shopping complexes had replaced just about all of the state-run stores. Privately run restaurants began to appear, replacing the workplace canteens as sites of eating outside the home. Entertainment forms proliferated, with movie theaters, bowling alleys, miniature golf, and theme parks such as Disneyland vying for people's time and money.

The ubiquity of global brands such as Starbucks, McDonald's, WalMart, and Apple in China's urban centers makes it tempting to view consumption practices as following a universal development process, centered around an American model. Nonetheless "we cannot assume that all consumer revolutions are fundamentally alike or are converging toward the endpoint of the American model" (Garon and Maclachlan 3: 2006). As we see even in this greatly abridged history of China over the last sixty years, the Chinese state has not merely "stepped aside" to allow capitalists to flourish. Rather, since 1979, it has implemented policies to encourage the development of consumerism, viewing it as an engine for both economic growth and social stability – both of which it believed were necessary in order for the CCP to maintain its political power. After the Asian financial crisis of 1997, the CCP proposed a push for private housing to spur the real estate market, as well as promoting investment in telecommunications, tourism, entertainment, and health care (Li 2010). In 2002, then premier Zhu Rongji declared at the Ninth People's Congress the necessity to stoke consumer demand: "We need to eliminate all barriers to consumption by deepening reform and adjusting policies. We need to encourage people to spend more on housing, tourism, automobiles, telecommunications, cultural activities, sports, and other services and develop new focuses of consumer spending" (Otis 2012: 43). In 2011, the National People's Congress enacted China's 12th five-year plan, which included three main building blocks: a greater focus on jobs, urbanization to boost wages, and financing a social safety net that encouraged families to spend rather than save. From the 1990s onwards, the state sought to portray and encourage its citizens to be consuming individuals, yearning to be fulfilled (Yang 1997: 303).

In addition to its economic reforms, the Chinese state's family planning policies over the last three decades have also had an enormous impact on the nature of consumption. In 1978, the state initiated the One-Child Policy, aimed at curbing China's population growth for the sake of alleviating social, economic, and environmental problems. Whether the policy has actually achieved its environmental and economic goals is still being debated but what is undeniable is that it has had a profound effect on China's social structures. The first generation of so-called Singletons, born in the late 1970s and 1980s, has grown up entirely within the economic reform period, and this has deeply shaped their lifestyles. These Singletons are now in the workforce and having their own Singletons, creating multiple generations that have grown up without the large extended families of cousins, aunts, and uncles that have characterized traditional Chinese families.

What this means is that as they are growing up, all of their family's resources, from parents and two sets of grandparents, are singularly focused on these Singletons. They have become the sole repository of all the elders' hopes and dreams. Marketers have jumped on this convergence of the natural parental desire to give their children the very best, and the increased purchasing power parents have in post-Mao China, by pushing an ever-increasing number of products, services, and educational opportunities. Magazines, billboards, and TV commercials bombard parents with images of healthy, happy, successful children, thanks to having the best fortified milk products, toys, and electronics. Expenditures on children and their education is enormous, averaging 30–40 percent of a household's income, according to the majority of parents whom I have interviewed. These expenditures include after-school tutorials, extracurricular activities, and learning products such as computers. Those parents who can do so are increasingly sending their children abroad for their education, even buying homes in foreign countries to establish residency for the sake of their children's futures.

The story of China's consumer revolution centers around the first and second generations of Singletons, born in the 1980s and 1990s (the so-called *balinghou* and *jiulinghou* generations). Their values and practices have been molded in a consumerist milieu very different from that which their parents and grandparents experienced, whose own upbringings were shaped by drastically different ideologies. Singletons themselves characterize their own lives in multiple ways. They see themselves as unique yet lonely, individualistic yet burdened by too many expectations. They have come of age in an extraordinary period of transformation, and see their main opportunity and challenge in terms of navigating through a rapidly changing China without the benefit of elders or siblings who can guide them through experience.

Some social commentators warn that this convergence of hyper-consumption and the One-Child Policy has resulted in a thoroughly spoiled youth generation, dubbed the "little emperors and empresses," which has never had to share or deal with parents saying no. Childhood in China has become thoroughly commercialized, as not only parents but the children themselves are viewed as active, discerning consumers. Throughout this book, we will explore how Singleton identity and experiences shape consumption practices.

Another unique aspect of China's economic transition is the role of the internet. Half a billion people in China are online. Not only does China have more internet users than any other country in the world, it has the world's largest population of gamers, the world's second largest population of online shoppers (behind the USA), the world's most engaged online social networkers, and the world's largest number of smartphone users, who can access the internet while mobile. Another significant fact to note is the relative youth of people online in China. Sixty percent of Chinese netizens are under thirty, in contrast to the US, where the average age is 42 (Herold and Marolt 2011). Analysts predict that China will become the largest ecommerce market by 2015. The rapid growth of online shopping can be attributable to several factors. The first is increased access to the internet through not only PCs but also mobile devices. The second is the growing use of credit cards, which allows for online transactions. The third is the explosion of online commerce sites, selling everything from electronics to cosmetics to bottled water.

China's virtual landscape is, however, distinctly different from much of the rest of the developed world. Western media observers have been quick to criticize the Chinese state for its so-called "Great Firewall," which blocks common international internet destinations such as Google, eBay, Facebook, and Wikipedia, and searches involving key words such as "Falung Gong" or "democracy movement Tiananmen." In fact, much of the academic work on China's internet tends to focus on the question of whether it can become a true public sphere, or space of resistance against the state. However, what is less understood is the role of the internet as a site of consumer practices. It would be a mistake to conclude that the Great Firewall has resulted in an internet experience that is any less dynamic than elsewhere in the developed world. In fact, China's internet ecosystem has developed a rich and varied set of ecommerce, social media, gaming, and search engine alternatives that are, in many ways, more functionally advanced than the online services available in the West.

The developed economies of the USA, Western Europe, and Japan evolved their consumer cultures decades before the internet became ubiquitous. As such, online shopping evolved gradually, and often merely augmented deeply rooted practices in the offline world of brick and mortar shopping. In contrast, China's consumer revolution occurred during the very same historical period that computers and their virtual worlds became globally accessible. As Herold and Marolt argue, "The density of the Chinese experience of modernity – learning to live with a modern capitalism and rapid cyberization at the same time – while moving from a closed society to a more open one within a very short period of time, is reason enough to expect the Chinese experience to be unique" (2011: 26). As we will explore in the next chapter, consumption practices are so intertwined with online access that people view themselves as living in a hybrid, "virtu-real" world. Thus, when we consider economic development in China, the internet is not just another medium through which people consume, but rather, a critical catalyst for accelerating and shaping consumption practices.

One question that is top of mind for most China watchers is whether or not China's economic liberalization and improving standards of living will lead to greater desire for political freedom and participation. As will be explored in the chapters to come, consumer culture has sparked new forms of identity expression and bolstered people's sense of agency over their lifestyles and futures. However, while the relationship between the government and ordinary citizens was drastically altered after 1978, with more room for people to control their work, leisure activities, social relationships, and how they spent their discretionary income, the state, nonetheless, retained its substantial authoritarian powers. The question remains whether or not increased consumption is a catalyst for social empowerment. The phenomenon is complex. Chinese individuals exert their voices and rights as consumers while at the same time maintain awareness of the boundaries their authoritarian government upholds.

APPLYING CONSUMPTION THEORY

Even this very brief historical examination reveals that the context within which consumption practices have developed in China differs significantly from the more mature consumer cultures of the USA, Western Europe, and Japan. How, then, does an examination of consumption in China contribute to our general understanding of universal consumer patterns? What about the consumer experience in China is universal, what is unique, and what theoretical frameworks can we apply to help us compare what is happening in China to what we have observed elsewhere?

The foundational studies that continue to shape consumption theory have, to a large extent, been based on Western European and North American societies. This is of course no accident, as these countries have had the longest histories of consumption-oriented economies with more or less stable political and economic systems based on modern forms of capitalism. China's consumer revolution is based on some very different structural factors, as we have seen in the brief historical overview. Nonetheless, many of the foundational consumption frameworks are appropriate starting points for our analysis. The goal of this section is not to provide a comprehensive review of consumption theory, for the literature set is too broad and too rich for this to be feasible. Rather, I would like to explore the key questions that have shaped the field, in order that we may understand what is happening in China in relation to the most enduring theoretical frameworks in the academic literature.

Who creates and controls consumer culture? This question is at the heart of consumption theory. In the now classic work *Capital*, Marx described how the relationship between people and the objects that they buy underwent an enormous transformation as societies transitioned from traditional to capitalistic economies (1990). Marx referred to this loss of connection to the origins of a product as a sense of alienation. Workers became alienated because they no longer controlled the process or design of what they were making. Consumers became alienated because they did not have a connection to the origin of what they acquired. In this historical view, Marx underscored the transition of objects from goods to commodities. Human relations between buyer and seller were recast as economic relations between objects. He called this phenomenon commodity fetishism. While Marx's work had far-reaching influence on consumption theory, his focus was actually more on production in terms of people's roles either as owners or workers. Consumption practices were viewed primarily in terms of alienation and fetishism. In other words, Marx portrayed consumers as passive players, who merely accepted the conditions that capitalists created. The principles of commodification will be central to our analysis of everyday life in China.

In *The Practice of Everyday Life* (1984), Michel de Certeau argued that people are not passive recipients of meanings that producers create, but rather, they create their own meanings around commodities through everyday decisions and actions. He points out that in a closer look at the tactics people employ in their everyday lives, we can begin to uncover the way in which ordinary people potentially subvert the meanings that corporations seek to define for them. He called these the "tactics of consumption," giving rise to a more agent-oriented view of how consumers act. Scholars shifted from a framework of alienation to one in which consumption was viewed as a democratic exercise, in which individuals could invent and reinvent themselves through their consumer choices. Instead of mass conformity, the postmodern scholars emphasized the use of commodities to construct individual, self-realized, resistant, and creative selves. The new agency-focused literature highlighted the ways in which people played with gender, ethnicity and subordinated identities, challenging and undermining structures of social domination. Consumption was no longer positioned as something negative, a submission to the will of the corporations, but rather, as a space for pleasure, escape, enjoyment, and possibly even liberation. Consumers were thus depicted in terms of their resistant, liberatory, and creative tendencies (Schor and Holt 2000). Identities and lifestyles, as seen through the lens of consumption, are dynamic and constantly changing (Arnould et al., 2004).

Consumption theory tends to focus on the tensions between structure and agency. Do producers (or capitalists) control consumption practices, as Marx would argue? Or do consumers engage in forms of agency through everyday tactics, as de Certeau and postmodern theorists would argue? While the literature is filled with examples from both ends of the spectrum, more current studies tend to agree that a range of dynamics is at work. Consumers operate within the structures presented to them as well as occasionally subvert or overcome such constraints. In his business focused book, Tom Doctoroff (2012) argues that Chinese consumers are attempting to stand out within the constraints of social norms – "standing out by fitting in," as he calls it. Michael Griffiths' work also tackles the question of whether Chinese consumers are truly capable of expressing individuality within the norms of social conformity, and illuminates areas in which consumers work within and beyond structure (2013).

A framework for understanding consumption in China, however, must include a third "actor" alongside the producers and consumers

– and that is the state. This tripartite relationship creates a constant push and pull of often differing agendas, continually shaping and reshaping China's unique consumption landscape. The relationships between the three players are, as we will see, complex, and who has the "upper hand" is not always consistent across contexts. Corporations are often beholden to the state in terms of their access to the market. As we will see in this book, the CCP can and does restrict some global companies, such as Google, from entering China without stringent conditions. Nonetheless, the state's influence has receded dramatically in the last two decades, replaced by new ideologies of cosmopolitanism and luxury which the global brands embody. In terms of the relationship between the state and consumers, the former has undoubtedly shaped the consumption experiences of a generation through its implementation of the One-Child Policy and its heavy hand in controlling the internet. Nonetheless, we also see consumers increasingly challenging the state, and in particular, the corruption among CCP officials, and such challenges have begun to affect policy. The relationship between producers and consumers is equally fraught with contradictions and complexities. On the one hand, we will see throughout this book that people's daily lives, including the way they raise their children, define gender norms, and shape their home environments, are immensely influenced by global corporations selling products, services, and lifestyles. On the other hand, we see consumers resisting the power of corporations through boycott campaigns and online exposés of faulty products.

A second key question which has shaped the consumption literature is *how social distinctions are created and experienced*. Perhaps the most seminal study comes from Thorstein Veblen, who drew upon turn-of-the-century American social practices. In *The Theory of the Leisure Class* (1899), he argued that in modern society, wealth, rather than military prowess, had become the basis of social status. Yet it was not always obvious how much wealth people had. Thus, the display of objects and the air of an idle lifestyle became the primary means of communicating status. Veblen coined the term "conspicuous consumption" to indicate that consumption acts were not just about fulfilling individual needs and desires, but about communicating to others one's place in the social hierarchy. His related concept of "conspicuous leisure" referred to the observable practice of spending significant amounts of time pursuing pleasure, as opposed to work, as a sign of higher social status.

Pierre Bourdieu refined Veblen's definition of social distinction based primarily on the acquisition of status-bearing goods. He argued that "good taste," and not just how much one spent on goods, also contributed to status. He differentiated several different forms of capital, which indicated one's position in society. "Cultural capital" referred to one's education, knowledge, and upbringing, which could all be viewed in terms of status. "Social capital" referred to one's group affiliations and social circles, and the influence or prestige that these groups represent (1984).

Jean Baudrillard, often associated with postmodern thought, inspired not only academics but marketing professionals with his work on the symbolic value of commodities. He argued that the prevalent, Marxian inspired definition of commodities, which included use-value (an object's function) and exchange-value (an object's monetary value), oversimplified people's needs. By arguing that objects also embodied a third type of value, which he called the "sign value," he brought a psycho-cultural perspective to Marx's materialistic framework. Sign values referred to the values that users, corporations, or marketers constructed around objects, which may have nothing to do with their actual functional use (2006). Corporate marketers have based their practices on Baudrillard's central insight into the symbolic value of otherwise indistinguishable commodities, expressed through a product's brand story.

Amy Hanser's *Service Encounters: Class, Gender, and the Market for Social Distinction in Urban China* (2008) and Eileen Otis' *Markets and*

Bodies: Women, Service Work, and the Making of Inequality in China (2012) both explore the social distinction practices associated with female service workers. In doing so they move beyond focusing on just a production or just a consumption perspective, effectively showing how the two are tied together in the everyday practices of service workers in China's new five-star hotels and luxury shopping malls.

Like Hanser and Otis, I will explore how consumers in China conceptualize their own desires and aspirations through social distinction practices. Mark Liechty's call to treat class as a process rather than a fixed endpoint offers an important theoretical foundation (2003). Social distinction practices in China have gone through a remarkable transformation over the last three decades. The CCP effectively dismantled all older forms of status when it took over the country in 1949. The former elite were stripped of their wealth, re-educated in the countryside, and otherwise dethroned from their social positions in the name of eradicating class differences. A new elite formed around Communist Party affiliations, but this was in political power only. The general population has not come to view this political elite as a source of inspiration for how to build status themselves. In fact, one of the most pressing socio-political problems is citizen discontent with the wealth and privilege associated with corrupt party leaders. Consequently, consumers in China – and young people, in particular – do not feel that they have an established and respected elite class to look up to when it comes to matters of status building.

The One-Child Policy, and the emergence of the world's first-ever generation of Singletons, is a fundamental part of the tremendous social change the country has seen over the last few decades. Being only children in a society of only children presents enormous amounts of adjustment and strain on the family structure. For the first generation of Singletons, now entering their thirties and early forties, there are no existing models to help them make sense of what they are experiencing. Their parents and grandparents do not have the benefit of prior experience as well. Instead of looking to their elders or an established elite, they are looking globally for ideas, drawing upon a "mashup" of ideas as well as their own imaginations to create emerging social distinction practices.

A third key question that shapes consumption theory is *how consumption shapes social ties*. Michel Maffesoli's concept of neo-tribes provides a foundational perspective on emerging forms of sociality as it relates to consumption (1996). The concept refers to affiliations based on everyday life events as opposed to "traditional" ties of kinship and geographical community. Neo-tribes are by nature spontaneously formed and often transient and impermanent. They may form around hobbies or passions. Seth Godin and others who study corporate branding techniques have noted the rise of neo-tribes based on brand affiliations (2008).

In China, as we will see throughout this book, relationships based on a common passion for a particular brand, such as Jeep or Disney, characterize emerging social ties. Consumers connect emotionally and pragmatically to certain luxury products that represent the kinds of lifestyles they aspire towards. Beyond Maffesoli's original conception, however, China's neo-tribes take on particular characteristics due to the use of the social media sites such as QQ to foster and reinforce virtual ties. This book explores how social identities are fostered and expressed across both online and face-to-face contexts.

Communing with brands and likeminded consumers in shopping spaces has thus become a significant form of leisure in China. Once considered trivial and not a reflection of "real" culture, which was always cast as high culture, shopping finally became a topic of academic study in the 1980s. Before then, the production-centric view of consumption had trivialized shopping as a dumbed down form of cultural practice. When the focus shifted to consumption as an equally important aspect of economic practice, academics brought shopping into focus as an integral part of not just consumption studies but cultural studies in general (Gottdiener 2000a). Shopping malls and other spaces of consumption have become serious, legitimate geographies of academic study (Shields 1992; Ritzer 2010). The relationship between place and identity formation became a salient focus in consumption studies (Miller et al. 1998; Friedman 1994).

Work on spaces in the USA, in particular, has focused on the proliferation of suburban malls, the gentrification of city, and the development of urban entertainment centers (Zukin 2004). George Ritzer argues that new spaces of consumption can be thought of as "cathedrals of consumption" – that is, they are structured as places where people go to practice their "consumer religion" through connecting with each other and participating in meaningful activities (2010: 7). In addition to malls, places such as themed environments (e.g. Las Vegas casinos, Hard Rock Cafés) offer clues in terms of the global nature of consumption (Rojek 2000: 66). Daniel Miller's work is particularly noteworthy in his attention to shopping as an activity whose primary meaning derives from the family relationships it helps produce and reproduce. As he argues, "Objects are social relations made durable" (1998: 19).

A fourth key question that has begun to shape consumption theory in more recent years is *how the internet affects consumer experiences.* While technology is gradually making its way into consumption theory, there is an entrenched tendency to view anything that happens on the internet as secondary to activities in the "real" world. But as is explored in this book, the internet is not just a tool to make commerce more efficient. It has also become an integral part of the social and emotional experience of consumption. Access to social media on mobile phones, the ability to share photos and thoughts instantaneously, and the constant sharing of everyday moments create what I call a "virtu-real" consumer landscape. People – especially younger Chinese who grew up with internet access – constantly move back and forth between interactions in the physical, face-to-face world, and interactions in the online world. They do not distinguish one as more authentic or important than the other and, in fact, believe that one without the other would make an experience incomplete.

The internet has also been explored from the perspective of the role it plays in the development of a public sphere in China (Herold and Marolt 2011; Shirk 2011). Jürgen Habermas' definition of the public sphere as a space of discussion, dissent, and potentially political action that stands independent of the state and the church is typically used as a benchmark for evaluating the state of China's democratic processes (1989). One of the most influential scholars who has deeply explored China's economic transformations through the perspectives of its citizens is Deborah S. Davis (1995, 2000, 2005, 2006). Her work focuses on the potential for a true civil society to emerge out of China's consumer revolution, particularly in urban areas where homeowners and other consumer groups are experimenting with resistance against state and local governmental regulations. Davis' work builds on a large body of theory in an adjacent field, which is focused on the concept of the public sphere.

This book takes a different perspective by focusing not on what China has "yet" to develop, but rather, by exploring the role that the consumer sphere *does* play in terms of individual and group expression. Consumer culture in China has, nonetheless, created a space of discussion and debate. In what this book calls the "consumer public sphere," individuals negotiate meanings with the state as well as with producers, seeking to define their identities not only as consumers, but as citizens. As Sharon Zukin argues, however, it is important to consider consumption on its own terms, as a space of significance that is neither completely free nor completely democratic (2004). Censorship of political discussions on social media, the banning of certain books and magazines critiquing the CCP, and the arrests of prominent artists and academics who call for democratic processes are all used as evidence to argue that China has not yet developed a "true" public sphere.

What is clear even in this very perfunctory look at the literature on consumption and its applicability to China is that it encompasses more than just the functional acquisition of goods on the market. So much of what defines and affects human behavior has some connection to market exchange, whether it is choosing the right baby food or planning the perfect wedding. As Don Slater argues:

> Even the most trivial objects of consumption both make up the fabric of our meaningful life and connect this intimate and mundane world to great fields of social contestation . . . Consumer culture is largely mundane, yet that mundanity is where we live and breathe, and increasingly so as we sense that the public sphere of life has become a consumable spectacle that is ever more remote as a sphere of direct participation. "Consumer culture" is therefore a story of struggles for the soul of everyday life, of battles to control the texture of the quotidian. (1997: 3–4)

The literature on consumption thus encompasses more than just an exploration of the acquisition and use of goods and services. When people consume, they also express who they are or want to be, the nature of their familial and peer relationships, their current or aspirational status, and how engaged they are with the world outside their immediate social circles. In other words, consumption is not easily disentangled from the other parts of life. Even in work and family life, we consume. We engage in activities such as "dressing for success," taking up golf to impress our colleagues, or engaging in power lunches. Likewise, families may solidify their bonds with a day at the mall, a trip to the movies, or through taking a Disneyland vacation. When we consider all of the things we consume – food, clothing, technology, media, education, leisure activities – it becomes difficult to clearly define where consumption ends and "the other" parts of life begin. "The act of consumption, which was once so exceptional an act in lives dominated by laborious production, is now commonplace and incessant. We are all in the market all the time" (Hine 2002: 59).

Likewise, in using the term "consumers," theorists of consumption are not just referring to the point when people take out their wallets and make a transaction with cash or credit cards. Rather, from an anthropological point of view, our roles as consumers are, in modern society, increasingly inseparable from our other roles as parents, children, teachers, professionals, and teenagers. By calling someone a consumer, what we indicate is that they are actively crafting their own meanings, identities, and lifestyles through the self-conscious choices they make in terms of what to spend their money on. They exercise choice in expressing their own tastes and preferences, and they use consumption to differentiate and affiliate. As consumers, people seek to control the messages about themselves that are broadcast to others.

The overarching themes in consumption literature summarized in this section are explored throughout this book from the perspective of Chinese consumer experiences. The concluding section of each chapter examines how theory can be applied to what is actually happening in China. The final chapter in this book returns to the question of what is global and what is unique about China's consumer revolution. The goal of incorporating theoretical discussions along with real-world examples and stories is to help us understand what is universal and what is particular about the formation of consumer cultures around the world. By validating, tweaking or reconceptualizing these frameworks, theory remains useful and dynamic – explanatory rather than constraining.

Furthermore, an exploration of both the universalities and particularities of China as a case study may help us better understand what is happening or could happen in other non-Western developing economies such as Vietnam, Burma, Cuba, and some emerging markets in Latin America and Africa. As the people and the governments of these countries continue to work out their own paths towards "modernity,"

China is an appealing model to emulate – an alternative to the models of Western democracy and capitalism. Whether these states develop similar configurations of power between themselves, their citizens, and the capitalists that seek to commoditize more of everyday life, is the subject of other studies. Nonetheless, what we can say is that consumption practices never "simply" come into being. Consumer culture is not a fixed entity but a process that is continually shifting. The how, what, and why's of consumption reflect the continual push and pull between governing forces, capitalists, and the people who seek to make their lives better through the purchase of goods and services.

HOW THIS BOOK IS STRUCTURED

This book is structured around multiple different facets of consumer culture in China. Chapter 2, "Spaces," focuses on the new landscape of consumption – the transformation of China's public spaces into leisure-oriented consumer destinations, and the replacement of state-owned stores with modern, glitzy malls and hypermarkets. In addition, I also examine the online consumption spaces of ecommerce and social media sites. As this chapter will demonstrate, consumers do not draw borders between "virtual" and "real," and in fact move seamlessly between these different spaces as they consume.

Chapter 3, "Status," explores the remarkable transformation from the ideal of a classless socialist society under Mao Zedong to the celebration of social distinctions today. We examine what class means from the perspective of consumers themselves, and delve into the ways they define social superiority through conspicuous consumption, luxury brand affiliations, expressing upward mobility, and overt displays of one's social networks.

Chapter 4, "Lifestyles," goes beyond the things people want to consume to explore the experiences they hope to have and embody. The emerging values around indulgence, self-fulfillment, and self-expression stand in stark contrast to the communal and self-sacrificial values of the past. Neo-tribes based on product and brand affiliations are supplanting older types of affiliations. Travel and becoming cosmopolitan subjects have become key aspirations for China's consumers.

Chapter 5, "Commodification," explores how areas of life that were once relatively untouched by market exchange have become fertile ground for corporations seeking to embed their products and services into ever-more parts of consumers' lives. Gender identities, child rearing, familial celebrations, and the private recesses of one's home are increasingly shaped and influenced by consumerism, as people find their choices both alternately expanded and constricted by what they are being sold.

Chapter 6, "Awareness," focuses on growing consumer activism against the negative consequences of consumption. Environmental degradation, loss of traditional values, and corrupt business practices leading to unsafe products are all areas that consumers are attempting to change through collective action. This chapter examines the role of online communities, in particular, in fostering civil awareness and power, and explores the question of whether China has or can develop a true public sphere of protest and democracy.

Chapter 7, "Consumption with Chinese Characteristics," circles back to the question of what is universal and what is unique about China's consumer revolution. I summarize which dynamics in China reflect global theory, and also highlight key characteristics that differ from the assumptions within these widely accepted frameworks.

The chapters in this book can be read in any order, as each one explores consumption in China from a different angle, as opposed to each one building on the last one. In some ways these chapters can be thought of as the proverbial blind man's hands on the elephant. Each view illuminates something different. Each view may even contradict the others in some way. However, when taken together and seen as a whole, they create an image that is both cohesive yet complex – like the elephant itself. The endless joy and frustration for those who study China is that it is such an enormous place that any study, no matter how long a period of time it encompasses or how comprehensive it may seem, is only a snapshot. This snapshot will, I hope, give readers a sense of the unprecedented economic, social, and political transformations that are shaping everyday lives in China today.

2 Spaces

Xiao Xiao, aged 54, vividly remembered her first purchase experience.

> When I was a little child, my deepest childhood memory was buying a popsicle for 4 cents. Back then, my ma had no money to spare, so this was a special treat. While standing at our gate, waiting for the popsicle vendor, I could hear the sound of his wooden carton getting knocked around on the back of his bicycle. I ran as fast as I could to meet him. When I got my popsicle, I was prouder than words could describe. I let my good friends have a lick, while the other children looked on jealously.

When we first met, Xiao Xiao had recently retired, and lived by herself in a compact apartment in the Huangpu district of Shanghai. Her community was made up of retirees, who shared activities every evening such as playing table tennis in the common room. She studied piano with her newfound free time, and learned how to use a computer. Her favorite activity was going online to chat with friends via QQ. Traveling was her passion, and she was hoping to take her elderly parents on a trip to Thailand later that year. Xiao Xiao played "auntie" to the grand-children in the neighborhood, spoiling them with her extra change so they could buy soft ice-cream cones at the McDonald's down the street.

> Although I am not wealthy, life has improved compared to the period under Chairman Mao. At that time, even the richest people did not

have a lifestyle equal to that of ordinary people today. Back then, we did not own any electrical appliances. We didn't have access to a rich cultural life. My whole family of six people lived in a 15-square-meter apartment. Nowadays, the average area for each person is 30 square meters. And there was never enough food. We could only get goods through ration tickets. In the past, we got what we needed from the state. When the economy started to open up, we bought things from street vendors and in wet markets, where we bargained for goods. Today, we buy things in big, clean shops like WalMart, where you can choose from ten or more options for anything. Even the ordinary person can buy things from all over the world here in Shanghai.

Xiao Xiao expressed her sense of change over time through comparing shopping in the past and in the present. Now in her mid fifties, she remembered the scarcity of the past, contrasting that with the choice and abundance of WalMart. The themes in her narrative are common among people in her generation. At the center of these narratives is the theme of transformation. On one end of the spectrum is the perception that China, as a nation, is transforming into a global superpower. The 2008 Olympics is viewed as the nation's entrance onto the world stage. On the other end of the spectrum is the perception that individual lifestyles are changing. People consistently point to the opportunities for work, education, and travel they have today that were unimaginable a generation ago. Most of all, people describe the transformation in the consumer landscape – the proliferation of new kinds of places where they can shop, eat, and be entertained. These new spaces of consumption are central to people's experiences of China's economic transformation, and they become sites where individuals express the changes in their own lives.

This chapter explores the transformation of China's spaces of consumption and the role these spaces play in people's own sense of change. By "spaces of consumption," I include the physical places where people walk, browse, shop, eat, socialize, and play – in other words, the restaurants, shopping malls, hypermarkets, and entertainment centers that increasingly make up China's urban centers. I also include virtual spaces – online destinations such as ecommerce sites and social media. As such, this exploration of spaces looks not only at physical constructs, but also the social constructs that spaces can engender (Benjamin 1999; Gottdiener 2000b; Massey 2005). When people choose particular spaces over others, they are also choosing to engage in different sets of meanings. Spaces of consumption thus become staging grounds for the expression of social distinction, self-identity, and familial relationships.

URBAN COMMERCIALIZATION

"To write about urbanization in China is to traffic in superlatives" (Campanella 2008). For visitors, like myself, who return year after year, it can be bewildering to find once quiet neighborhoods developed into office buildings and other commercial sites. At the start of the reform period in 1979, Shanghai's skyline had no skyscrapers. Today, the city boasts twice as many as New York. In 2012, China had 19 out of 20 of the world's fastest growing cities (Thompson 2012); 691 million lived in China's cities, representing 10 percent of the population of the entire world, and the CCP's stated goal is to increase the proportion of those living in the cities from the current 47.5 percent to 51.5 percent by 2015 (*People's Daily Online* 2011).

Manufacturing as well as housing began shifting to the urban periphery, making way for high-rent facilities such as top-end hotels, condos, and banks. China is expected to have over 4,000 shopping malls by 2015 (Lin 2013). WalMart owns over 370 stores in over 120 cities in China. IKEA has opened a dozen stores across the nation after introducing its flagship store in Beijing in 2006, which received more visitors in 2011 than any other IKEA store in the world. Starbucks has 100 stores in Beijing and over 700 country-wide, and expects China to be its second largest market outside the USA by 2014 (Wall 2013). In 2013, McDonald's had over 2000 outlets, but is still behind KFC, with its 3200 stores (Gao 2011). While the early wave of urban commercialization efforts focused on the big coastal cities of Beijing and Shanghai, the next decade of growth is expected to occur in China's second- and third-tier cities.

China's city centers have transformed from sites of manufacturing and production, under Chairman Mao, to sites of consumption and imagination. They are, as cultural critic Walter Benjamin described in his exploration of Parisian arcades in the nineteenth century, not just spaces where money and goods are exchanged, but also spaces of representation (1999). One of Shanghai's versions of the arcade is Nanjing Road, a five-mile stretch through the city which ends at the waterfront near the historic Bund district. People of all ages flock there to walk, see, and be seen. Couples walk arm in arm, fashion-conscious young women teeter on high heels, and domestic tourists speaking various dialects marvel at the neon and crowds that only dissipate near midnight. The atmosphere here is a festive mix of people shopping and window shopping. These destinations are, as George Ritzer puts it, cathedrals of consumption where people gather to worship their favorite brands alongside an equally dedicated community (2010). Even such historical spaces as Tiananmen Square in Beijing are now surrounded by fast-food restaurants and luxury boutiques. For many years, Beijing's most revered historical site, the Forbidden City, even hosted a Starbucks, until public outcry shut it down.

Pre-1990, the consumer landscape was dominated by state-owned stores featuring domestic products and some Eastern European items. Given the context of scarcity that had pervaded consumer lives throughout the 1950s to 1980s, there was little "need" to create interest around products through advertising and alluring packaging. People bought what was available, and this often meant few choices between manu-facturers and styles. Today, the availability of a vastly wider range of global products has precipitated the introduction of branded shopping experiences into China. Branding, in essence, differentiates otherwise functionally similar products through symbolism and narratives that marketers hope will connect to consumers' aspirations. As Jean Baudrillard argued, commodification reaches its apogee once consumers imbue objects with sign values (2006).

We will explore in greater detail the roles of branded products in the chapter exploring social status. For our current discussion on spaces of consumption, it is important to note that the commercialization of the city has also entailed an ever-increasing number of branded spaces. These include luxury boutiques such as Louis Vuitton and Shiseido, five-star hotel brands such as The Four Seasons and Shangri-La, Western fast-food outlets such as McDonald's and KFC, sports stores such as Nike and Adidas, and shopping markets such as WalMart and Carrefour.

These brands embody several important meanings for shoppers in China. The first, most fundamental meaning is trust. In my own research on shopping habits, I heard people emphasize over and over again the fact that even if goods are more expensive in these branded stores, they feel a peace of mind knowing that what they buy is "guaranteed." What they mean by that is the assurance they feel based on the global nature of these brands. This assurance stands in contrast to the hit and miss experiences of pre-1990 shopping, when it was a given among the masses that domestically produced goods had to be checked thoroughly before purchasing, and that consumers had few, if any, rights vis-à-vis the retailers.

WalMart, for example, is often mentioned for being the antithesis of the state-owned stores of the past. The way WalMart is talked about by consumers in China may surprise the average American shopper. In the USA, WalMart typically represents inexpensive shopping for the masses, a place that prioritizes everyday deals over style or fashion. Few in the USA would point to the ambiance or experience of WalMart as particularly inspiring or enchanting. In fact, it is often disparaged by more upscale shoppers for being an unattractive place, with artless shelving, unattractive lighting, and underpaid staff. In China, however, consumers view WalMart in very different terms. For them, the brand embodies modernity and all that goes along with it: cleanliness, variety, and the delight of having not just a few but multitudes of choices. They mention the good service, the fun of sampling items in the store, and the peace of mind they feel when they see the retail workers wearing cloth nose and mouth covers. WalMart represents all of the promises of China's consumer revolution.

These new consumer spaces give shoppers in China more than just a place to exchange money for goods – they become experiences in and of themselves. Zhu Long, a middle-aged professional and father of a 6-year-old girl, described a recent visit to the Apple store, where he was doing more than just trying out new products. He was, in essence, communing with the Apple brand.

> I went to the Apple store on Nanjing Lu. It was so crowded, as usual. Everybody was there, playing around with different things, having fun exploring. I stopped at one of the iPads and experimented with the different apps. It was perfect. I used my mobile phone to take a photo of this scene. I really want to get an iPad and make it the center of our entertainment system at home. Since Steve Jobs's death, this wish has become stronger. I could have just ordered an iPad online but I like being around other Apple fans, and seeing the enthusiasm of the people who work there.

Similarly, Shen Yu, a young, unmarried professional, describes the décor of a restaurant, and not the food, as the main reason why she goes there.

We had lunch at Xinbeile Restaurant. The food is tasty but I don't usually feel satisfied with the dainty portions. However, I love going there with my female colleagues because the décor is so beautiful. I feel transported into another world. I love the way they use flowers to partition the tables, the oil paintings, and the delicate droplights over each table. I feel like we're in a Renaissance scene.

Zhu and Shen are not just consuming products in these spaces, but are also engaged in the consumption of space itself (Gottdiener 2000b).

The transformation of China's urban centers into more than just collections of stores, but into entertainment destinations, means that even those with limited spending capacity can participate. Teenagers purchase ice-cream cones and gather in groups outside McDonald's on Nanjing Lu. The ice-cream cone is their price of entry, so to speak. Likewise, young women describe spending their weekends going from mall to mall, window shopping. Even though they cannot afford most of the items, they can afford a cup of coffee from the food court, and that in and of itself makes them feel like they have just as much permission to be there as the luxury class with their high-limit credit cards. I have observed for years now that in city centers, most pedestrians carry branded shopping bags, featuring logos such as Shiseido, Luis Vuitton or Benetton. I originally assumed they had all just come from buying something at such stores. But in a recent study I did on shoppers' habits, I discovered that many people re-use branded shopping bags to hold their lunches or wallets and mobile phones. Carrying such bags while walking through the city gives them a sense of belonging – they can walk through any boutique or mall and the bag announces that they are legitimate consumers. So emotionally satisfying is this strategy of announcing one's belonging that counterfeit branded shopping bags have also made their way into China's consumer culture.

Urban spaces of consumption have also come to play central roles in the transformation of leisure time in China. Zhu Long, the Apple fan, acknowledged that he neglects his family on weekdays, as he stays at his office late, then often has dinner with friends or goes to work out at a gym. But he makes up for his neglect on the weekends, when he typically takes his family to the mall. "The weekend is a time of happiness and togetherness." His 6-year-old daughter, wife and mother-in-law look forward to seeing the sights. The city center is a good place for everyone. They typically start off with having lunch together somewhere – maybe Japanese noodles or McDonald's. Then his wife and mother-in-law go off and see a movie. He takes his daughter to the arcade in the mall. "There were a lot of games and my girl wanted to try every one. The paper game money was finally exchanged for some gifts." Afterwards they grab a snack at Burger King – the girl's favorite is soft serve ice-cream. Then the two make their way to Toys R Us. "Although she has a lot of toys already, she always finds something new to want. It reminds me of a saying – the rice in others' cookers is more delicious." Zhu Long described their most recent weekend outing in this way: "She was very happy, and these days, I find my own happiness is based on her moods. When I can do these things with her, I feel like a good father."

During the years of Mao's regime, not only was production controlled in the sense that what people did for a living was organized and dictated by the state, but also what one did during one's free time was also subject to state control. During the height of the Cultural Revolution, all leisure activities were planned by the work unit, or *danwei*, and while not always explicit, attendance was required in order to demonstrate one's support of a "right" way of life. Movies, sporting events, and dances were all organized by the *danwei*, and students and workers were expected to attend, regardless of what they really wanted to do. People who did not participate risked being criticized as not on board with the socialist mindset. Throughout the Cultural Revolution, people were warned that hobbies outside those organized by the *danwei* were potentially poisonous. Movies, books, and plays that did not reflect the CCP's ideology began to disappear. During the Cultural Revolution, state intrusion into people's daily lives became so pronounced that there was no true demarcation between "private time" and "public time." All leisure activities had to reflect Maoist propaganda and state ideology. Leisure activities were thus highly politicized (Wang 1995).

In post-socialist China, private lives are, for the most part, no longer subject to the kind of intense state control that they had been in previous decades. How people spend their leisure time is now at their own discretion. Zhu Long's description of his typical weekend is not unique. In a survey I conducted on non-work activities, I found that the number one weekend leisure activity among families was visiting a shopping center together. The centrality of shopping to family time highlights several transformations in family dynamics. The first is the shift from politicized to privatized leisure time. In pre-reform times, the state organized children's entertainment activities, which typically revolved around the *danwei*, and focused on learning or expressing adherence to socialist principles. The second key transformation is the development of the idea of weekends for leisure and, by extension, consumption. Previously, the weekend was not demarcated in China as a non-productive time. This growing norm of dedicating the weekend to family and leisure reflects the state and corporations' desires to increase consumption activities. The third transformation is reflected in Zhu Long's sentiment around what it means to be a good father. In his narrative, shopping spaces are significant locations where familial relationships can be nurtured and expressed. Daniel Miller's work is particularly noteworthy in terms of the ethnographic attention paid to familial relationships and shopping practices. Shopping, he concludes, is not so much about buying things for other people but about being in relationships with those people (1998).

Urban development, however, is of growing concern to some. In 1978 China had 462 cities, compared to 655 by 2007 (*People's Daily* 2008). The urban population increased from 173 million in 1978 to 594 million in 2007 (Li 2010). Large portions of the city's traditional housing, or *hutong*, were razed to make way for high rises and shopping complexes. In *The Last Days of Old Beijing*, travel writer Michael Meyer documents the lives of people in the *hutong* he lives in, as well as the changes brought on by developments such as the construction of a WalMart and of course, preparations for the Olympics (2008). In the 1980s, there were over 2000 hutongs in Beijing. Today, there are only about 200 left. Numbers vary, but by some estimates, 1.5 million people were displaced in order to make way for construction in preparation for the Olympics (FlorCruz 2012).

Even the close to 600-year-old Forbidden City in Beijing has been transformed by commercialization. In 2000, Starbucks opened a store in the heart of China's number one tourist destination. Palace managers were looking to raise money to maintain the 178-acre complex. Critics, however, complained that the store was an inappropriate foreign symbol in the midst of one of China's greatest historical sites. The uproar finally resulted in the closing of the outlet in 2007. Following that closure, palace planners decided to cut down on the number of tourist shops in its grounds in order to maintain more of the authentic imperial-era appearance. In 2012, Starbucks opened a store near the Lingyin Temple in Hangzhou, eliciting similar protests. The temple was founded in AD 328, and the building has been a destination for pilgrims for over a thousand years. While some are calling for the closure of Starbucks, others have pointed out that the area near the temple has already been commercialized, with a KFC and several other stores already located on the commercial strip.

The rapidly changing urban landscape has some worried that China's cities are all becoming homogenized. Every urban center seems to have the same kinds of shopping malls, Western fast-food restaurants, and five-star international hotels. Inside such places, the feeling is virtually the same as being in any other modern city in Asia. Regional differences are diffused as a globalized consumer culture takes hold (Rojek 2000; Zukin 2004). Gottdiener (2000b) describes a kind of deterritorialization, as NYC becomes located in Las Vegas, and everywhere, themed environments erase local distinctions. Elsewhere, this has been called the "McDonaldization" of the cityscape, as global brands homogenize the experiences people have across spaces (Ritzer 2000).

NAVIGATING DIFFERENT SHOPPING EXPERIENCES

Despite these widespread consumer narratives of urban commercialization and experiential transformation, the shopping landscape remains complex and characterized by the continued presence of older shopping forms. Despite the growing ubiquity of places such as hypermarkets, wet markets continue to exist within neighborhoods. Small retail stores continue to operate. All throughout the cities, "black market" entrepreneurs compete with authentic, branded stores. In fact, sometimes these seemingly contradictory forms live side by side. While walking down Shanghai's Nanjing Road or Beijing's Wangfujin area, it is not uncommon to be approached by individuals covertly advertising counterfeit goods available on some side street.

In my own research, I have found competing perspectives. On the one hand, consumers of all ages celebrate the proliferation of places like WalMart, praising the new shopping spaces as both contributing to and symbolizing their own improving lifestyles. On the other hand, some older people note that while the new shopping experiences are impressive, they wish they could bargain over prices, the way they can in the non-branded spaces. "The price is the price in the shopping malls, you can't do anything about it," laments Xiao Xiao, the 54-year-old retiree we met earlier. While overpaying is certainly a concern for these older shoppers, the root of their dissatisfaction is actually the uniformity of the newer shopping experiences. For them, the wet markets and corner stores represent personalized interactions with sellers and producers (see Zukin 2004: 21 for discussion of replacing food markets with indoor stores). This interaction, for some older consumers, recognizes their own agency as shoppers with a voice, who have the right to haggle over prices, point out flaws, and affect the transaction in very fundamental ways.

In contrast, younger consumers in China tend to characterize these types of shopping experiences as untrustworthy and potentially dangerous. Wet markets or corner stores are places where they can get sick or get cheated. They view themselves as lacking the ability to navigate within such contexts. As one young woman put it, "I don't know how much things are supposed to cost. I fear I'll pay too much and get laughed at (by the vendor) behind my back. In a supermarket, I will not feel so stupid."

Consequently, younger consumers in China typically express a generation gap when I ask them about how they learn how to become good shoppers. People in their twenties and thirties say they typically have to figure things out for themselves or among their friends, for their parents and grandparents have little to teach them when it comes to shopping. In many cases, younger consumers feel they need to instruct their parents on what to expect, how to behave, and most of all, how to enjoy the new forms of shopping. Consequently, China's younger generation must look outside their families for help and mentorship in becoming "successful" consumers.

Retail workers play significant roles in this knowledge gap. Female shoppers, in particular, emphasize how important it is to interact with retailers. In my own observations, I have noticed a much more intimate kind of interaction between customers and sales associates in China than in consumer spaces like the USA, Western Europe, and Japan. Retailers recognize that their job is not just to present items but also to help the buyer navigate through potentially unfamiliar territory. When speaking with older customers, retailers often take the tone of a knowledgeable adult child, persuading the older person to trust the expertise that comes from their own, more "worldly" perspective. When speaking with peers, retailers often take the tone of fellow classmates or friends, who bring to life the product through relaying their own, personal experiences. Indeed, the role of the retailer is often not just as a facilitator but as a companion. Relatedly, shopping in China is rarely a solo activity. People nearly always shop with friends. When they do not, the retailer takes on that role – especially if both parties are female. The conversation and shared imagining about the product become important parts of the consumer's journey.

Learning even occurs in such mass retail environments as WalMart. This is particularly salient in the category of food, where consumption patterns have shifted tremendously over the last two decades, with Chinese families buying more milk and meat, and integrating more packaged foods into their diets. On a recent trip to WalMart near Beijing, I observed young female employees cheerfully handing out yogurt samples, encouraging customers to try flavors including red bean, lychee, and even gelatinous donkey skin. In a study about children's food, the parents I spoke with were emphatic about their belief that dairy products would help their children grow healthy and smart. Advertisements for milk products play on the idea that parents who buy their children such foods give them a boost in life. Service workers at places such as WalMart play a significant role in introducing parents and grandparents to these products, which are still relatively new to Chinese diets.

Patricia Pao, CEO of the Pao Principle, conducted one of the first, large-scale studies of luxury consumers in China. She has observed how beauty products are introduced to women in China. Beauty information was non-existent until the early 1990s. While Western women are generally initiated into beauty rituals by their mothers, Chinese women are dependent on outside sources for their beauty information because, when growing up, their mothers had no access to any of the products and practices available today. Cosmetics companies fill that void through featuring make-up consultants and fashion celebrities who mentor customers through in-store demonstration, blogs, and TV spots. Pao has observed that one particularly successful type of program is the "lunch-and-learn" session for secretaries and other "office ladies." It is thus no coincidence that, in China, "drugstore" cosmetics brands such as Maybelline and L'Oreal are sold alongside higher end brands such as Estee Lauder in Shiseido. Department store environments are well suited for the kind of education and mentoring that women are looking for in their quest to "personalize" themselves through adornment.

Gu Hui, a single woman and professional, describes such an encounter with a cosmetics guru:

> While shopping with my friend, I happened to see a stage set up at the front of the department store. Mr P (a well-known cosmetics expert featured on TV) was teaching women about make-up trends for autumn. There were a lot of girls gathered around. Mr P seemed very approachable. The lecture lasted for about 45 minutes. He taught us how to make our faces look smaller and how to choose foundation products that match our skin. And then they asked us questions to test our knowledge. I answered one question correctly and was rewarded with a DVD featuring Mr P. The atmosphere here was charged with excitement.

Opportunities for learning about new consumption practices also span physical and virtual contexts. Online bloggers have become celebrities followed by hundreds of thousands of people, instructing followers on everything from make-up to child care. "I follow bloggers who specialize in financial matters, women's issues, hair care, travel, and educating children. They give us relatively neutral and objective opinions and so much information we can't easily find elsewhere," says Gu Hui. The internet, along with more traditional forms of media such as TV and print, augment the in-store experiences to introduce consumers in China to new ways of transforming their own lives.

CONSUMING MODERN SPACES

In addition to shopping centers, restaurants are also sites of transformation. Twenty years ago, people's choices for eating out were minimal. They could spend a small fortune at the banquet halls, which typically served Party cadres. Or they could eat at the very modest state-run restaurants, which focused on serving up simple foods for cheap prices, without much thought about décor or service. Quick, "fast food" consisted of *hefan*, or boxed lunches, common outside train stations or other places domestic travelers were likely to want a quick and inexpensive meal. Prior to 1990, there were few restaurants in the big cities designed for mass consumption. For most people, eating out was extremely rare.

Today, China's biggest cities offer as many different restaurant experiences as other global cities around the world. In a study I conducted in 2012, consumers in China filled out detailed journals on their daily activities, including any instances that involved spending money or considering spending money. Among my thirty participants, eating out was by far the most common consumption activity. For the single, young professionals in particular, eating out was an almost daily obsession. Time at work was spent looking up restaurant reviews, deal-hunting, and instant messaging with colleagues in order to decide on where to go. My informants wrote, often passionately, about their experiences trying new cuisines and then sharing these experiences with others via social networking and restaurant review sites.

Foreign restaurants hold a particularly interesting meaning for consumers in China. For example, Western fast-food places are not, from the Chinese consumers' perspective, cheap and fast places to eat. Rather, they are valued for being clean, brightly lit, and featuring friendly, efficient service. This is in stark contrast to the surly service people were accustomed to in the state-run restaurants and work canteens. Consumers who frequent places like McDonald's in China are typically professionals, trendy hipsters, and well-educated youth. And unlike Western customers, who value the "fast" in fast food, consumers in China linger longer, even holding business meetings and romantic outings at such places. Eating foreign food has become an important way for upwardly mobile Chinese to enact their "middle classness" (see Yan 1997 and 2000 for more on the meanings behind Western fast-food restaurants in China).

Fiona Reilly, a food blogger who has toured China with her family in a motor home (a rare sight), has noticed the proliferation of what she calls "vaguely Western style brands," such as UBC coffee – which is in fact Taiwanese owned. UBC is decorated with large, baroque sofas, vintage clocks, and photos of Louis Armstrong. It has what Reilly calls a kind of "commodified nostalgia," but a distinctly Western one. As Reilly notes and I have observed in my own research among food trends in China, the food is often not the central focus of these Western-style cafés and restaurants. Rather, being in the space signifies an engagement with modern life. Shen Yu, the young female professional we met earlier who enjoyed places with a certain ambiance, articulated it this way:

> Western food like hamburgers tastes okay, although usually I prefer Chinese food. But I like going to KFC because that's where people of high quality (*suzhi*) go. You know these people will act properly in public, they will not spit on the ground, they will act with some sophistication. I prefer to be in this environment, and to be seen there by others.

As one mother put it to me when describing her habit of taking her child to McDonald's every week, foreign restaurants are a "window to the world." These new consumer spaces are not just clean and brightly lit, they represent new forms cultural knowledge. This mother says that she brings her 6-year-old to McDonald's so he can grow comfortable in a Western style setting. When he grows up, she argues, he can more easily interact with foreigners. Corporations, such as UBC Coffee, have discovered this fascination and play up their "foreignness," even if their origins are Asian.

Western restaurants are also settings where young people experiment with new lifestyles and identities. One young couple described the sense of freedom they felt in Starbucks, where they could hold hands and kiss. When I asked why they did not feel comfortable acting that way in Chinese restaurants or tea houses, they said that they felt compelled to act more "traditional" in certain places. The "modern," "Western" environment of Starbucks thus gives them a kind of permission to act differently. These emerging consumption spaces represent new forms of sociality and behavior. Not coincidentally, besides children and teens, the most frequent visitors to fast-food places are adult women. Eating out was not something that a woman or a group of women did just a few decades ago, as pre-reform restaurants privileged male consumers and family units. Today, foreign-style cafés and restaurants provide alternative contexts for women to participate in public life without the need to be seen with husbands, boyfriends, or families. Food consumption is not merely functional in nature but can also be analyzed as a symbolic system reflecting economic status, social identity, political power, and other lifestyle characteristics (Bourdieu 1984: 177–99).

Restaurants that represent modern Asian cultures – Japanese, Korean, Taiwanese – are also becoming popular as spaces that embody desirable consumer experiences. Taiwanese cuisine, in particular, has elicited a lot of interest from consumers in China, who flock to Taiwanese tea shops, noodle stands, and fast-food restaurants to experiment with the cuisine from a place that was, until the last few decades, a mystery to them. Interest in Korean cuisine is part of a larger "Korean Wave" phenomenon, in which Korean movie stars, pop music, and culture in general have become trendy in China. Japanese restaurants represent not just a different cuisine, but in some cases, a new aesthetic. Da Shan, an internet startup executive, related his delight over an experience at a Japanese restaurant in Shanghai called People Six.

> The decorations at People Six are designed by the Japanese minimalist master Miura Eichi, reflecting simple and modern styles. There aren't many things to eat there but every dish is like an art work. The place is usually filled with high-tier consumers, stars, business people, and artistic youth.

As we will explore further in the chapter on status, engaging with "global Asia" has become just as important in defining social status as engaging with the West.

REINVENTION OF SELF

As consumption theorists have long recognized, consumer behaviors and subjectivities are deeply intertwined. What is worn, displayed, used, and referenced are all vehicles for communicating one's sense of self to others. As such, from the perspective of consumption, identities are never fixed or singular, but rather, subject to reinvention, play, and continual transformation (Miller et al. 1998). Consumer spaces can thus be framed as stages for such identity experimentations (Hine 2002).

These new consumer spaces also encourage experimentation because they offer a sense of anonymity. Liu Guo Qiao, a 38-year-old teacher and mother, said:

I like large, comprehensive shopping malls and WalMart. I feel free there because no salesmen will follow me around. I often go shopping in clothing stores, shoe stores, and supermarkets in which the shop associates have to watch their own area because they can't follow me around. I can choose to ask them for help, but they will not take the initiative.

As Thomas Hine has argued

Retailing has profited mightily from one of the most potent inventions of the nineteenth century: anonymity. Getting lost amid strangers frees you from what others know and expect of you. It allows you to imagine being a different person. It invites you to wonder about the others in the crowd, and what they are thinking and dreaming. Being unknown offers a delicious freedom, the possibility that you can turn yourself into someone unexpected and surprising. All of these feelings encourage shopping. (2002: 126)

THE ONLINE LANDSCAPE

While the physical realm of consumption – shopping malls, restaurants, and entertainment centers – is the most visually apparent area of development, the growth of the virtual realm has been equally significant in the shaping of China's consumer culture. By virtual realm, I mean the online "spaces" in which people visit, play, seek out entertainment, socialize, and shop. The growth of and use of the internet in China is nothing short of remarkable. The penetration rate is at over 42 percent, up from 4.6 percent just a decade ago. Of the close to 600 million people online in China at the end of 2012, 420 million of them were regularly accessing the internet through mobile devices such as smartphones, and 300 million regularly engage in social media sites, which include blogs, social networking sites, and microblogs. The average time a netizen spends online is just over twenty hours a week. Reflecting the centrality of China's youth population, 30.4 percent of those online are between the ages of 20 and 29. China currently has just under 200 million online shoppers, surpassing the USA's 170 million. By 2015 it is estimated that the number of people shopping online in China will exceed 700 million, more than twice the total population of the USA. In terms of time, internet users in China spend at least 1.6 hours a week shopping online, and 46 minutes a day visiting social media sites. Among these users, 12 percent of total spending comes from internet shopping (China Internet Network Information Center 2013).

Despite the centrality of the internet to understanding China's consumer revolution, academic studies on the internet have tended to focus more on its potential role in developing a free public sphere in China. This stems from an academic preoccupation with the relationship between economic development and political freedom in China – or the general lack thereof. In the chapter "Aware," we will return to the question of how the state controls internet usage through censorship and blocking specific websites and search terms. Here, we will focus not so much on what the internet could be (from a Western point of view), but rather, what the internet actually is in China today. And from that perspective, the internet is a dynamic space of consumer experimentation, discovery, and sharing. China's virtual landscape is in fact vast and varied. Despite, or perhaps because of, the fact that the Chinese state has banned such internationally popular internet websites as Google, Facebook, and Wikipedia, domestic Chinese internet companies have filled those gaps with a variety of options that are often more innovative and functionally advanced than their Western counterparts. Below is a summary of some of the key players in the virtual world, as they will be referenced throughout the rest of this book.

In terms of online consumer sites, there are a plethora of options specializing in everything from technology to books to slightly used luxury goods. The biggest name in online commerce is, undoubtedly, *Taobao*, which is often compared with eBay as a platform for small businesses and individual entrepreneurs to open retail stores. *Taobao's Aliwangwang* service allows buyers and sellers to chat live via an embedded instant messaging service, facilitating trust in an otherwise anonymous space. *Dianping* is another popular site, featuring local reviews of restaurants, shops, and service providers. Younger internet users, in particular, delight in taking photos of dishes in restaurants using their mobile phones and sharing their opinions on *Dianping*. In addition to reviews, the site features daily deals and group purchase offers, similar to Groupon in the USA.

In terms of social media, microblogging refers to the posting of very short entries or updates on a blog or social networking site. Twitter, one of the most popular sites worldwide, has been blocked in China since 2009. China's versions are called *Weibo*, and similarly, allow 140 character messages (although because of the nature of the Chinese language, 140 characters can communicate a lot more than a 140 letter Tweet in English). There are a couple of significant *Weibo* players, including *Tencent Weibo*, which had 469 million users in 2012, *Sina Weibo*, which had 368 million, and *Netease Weibo* which had 36.5 million (Millward 2012). In addition to following friends, users in China follow celebrity bloggers who often advise on topics such as fashion, health, and cosmetics. Following brands and companies has also become popular, as consumers receive advance notice on special online deals. For example, when WalMart-backed retailer 360.com put its home appliances on sale, the CEO first announced it in a *Weibo* post.

Although Facebook is blocked in China, there is no dearth of functionally rich and widely used social networking sites. Some popular ones include *Kaixin* and *Renren*, which are similar in style and functionality to Facebook. The most widely used and the oldest social networking platform is QQ, owned by Tencent. QQ started off as an

IM client, but has developed into a multi-purpose portal that includes games, news, shopping, media, and blogging. It includes communication features such as video chat, and games such as the popular Stealing Vegetables, which required feed and care of one's avatars. QQ is especially popular with those outside the big cities, who may not have regular computer access, but can access the internet via the QQ app on their mobile phones. In fact, QQ occupies a special role in China as the oldest social networking site and the one used by the widest variety of Chinese consumers, from the rural and small town population to the urban university students (Hjorth and Arnold 2012). It is also the most common social networking site used by the older generations, who have adopted it as a means to keep in touch with children who may have moved away for school or work. QQ serves to link different platforms, media experiences, generations, and spaces (Koch et al. 2009).

China's virtual landscape is also rich with media content – always for free. *Tudou* and *Youku* are similar to YouTube in that they feature videos posted by users. Unlike YouTube, however, they feature full-length movies for free. Music, movies, and books are commonly free downloads, as China has yet to institute a consistently enforced digital rights management policy. Copyright violations are not enforced in China with the same discipline as they are elsewhere, and the casual shopper can easily find pirated DVDs of movies that are still in theaters, as well as all forms of pirated software.

In any discussion about China's internet usage, it is important to emphasize the enormous role that mobile phones play. Mobile apps for payment, price comparisons, finding restaurants nearby, reading reviews, posting photos on microblogging sites, ordering taxis, and finding out how friends have rated a place have all become commonplace ways to engage the virtual world while consuming in the physical world. Compared to the average urban resident in the USA, China's urban population is, as a whole, more advanced when it comes to mobile internet use in terms of the frequency of use and the variety of behaviors. From my own work with global companies, I know that in considering what the future will look like when it comes to mobile devices, product managers are just as likely to look to China as they are to the advanced economies of the West and Japan as models for inspiration.

HYBRID SPATIAL EXPERIENCES

Most academic studies on consumption in China focus on the so-called "real" world – that is, the physical world, or they focus on the potential of the virtual world for political expression and civil society. However, in my own research on the role of internet in China, I have found that consumers in China do not distinguish between virtual and real spaces when it comes to their daily consumer practices. Rather, they move seamlessly between the two throughout the day, initiating consumption in one realm and continuing it into the other. The virtual and the real are experienced as a continuum of consumer experiences. In fact, for many, consumer activities do not feel complete until both the physical and the virtual aspects are satisfied. I call these emerging forms of consumption "virtu-real" to signify the fact that consumers themselves have developed behaviors that span across both.

Gu Hui, the young female professional we met earlier, who was thrilled to meet Mr P at a mall event, is 24 years old, and works as a secretary in a finance company. When we met, she was not especially passionate about her work, but admitted it was a good first job to get out of college because she made a decent salary and her coworkers were fun to be around. Like other unmarried young professionals, she lived with her parents and so did not need to pay for most expenses. For the most part, she spent her salary any way she wanted to. Gu Hui described a typical work day:

While at work, my coworkers and I chatted on QQ about where we were going to have lunch. I looked on *Dianping* for group deals, and I found one for a Shabu Shabu place that was not far from our office. The reviews for the place were pretty good. The photos, especially the one for the beef soup, whetted my appetite. I shared the link on QQ with the group of four coworkers and we made our plans that way. Once we decided to go, I downloaded the coupon onto my mobile phone. When we met to go to the restaurant, I used my mobile phone to guide us to the place, which was about a ten-minute walk. The place was crowded but we got seated pretty quickly. The portions were good. I took photos of each one and posted them on *Weibo* along with a message about the group coupon. While eating I got fifteen comments from my network, who all said they were looking forward to trying the place too. I think delicious food brings us greater fun if we share with others, so I hope more people will go to the Shabu Shabu restaurant through my comments.

Gu Hui's description of lunchtime planning on a typical work day reflects the intertwined nature of virtual and physical consumption experiences. When I asked her where her colleagues sat, she said they were actually right next to her. Why didn't you just turn to them and have a face-to-face conversation about where to go to lunch, I asked. She giggled and replied as if it were the most obvious thing in the world that messaging as a group on QQ was "more fun," and that they could have the conversation over the course of the entire morning, sharing links and photos along the way. Plus, she admitted, they could look like they were doing work while they were in fact "dreaming about what to eat." However, the online component did not go away even when the group was on break from work. Once at the restaurant, they took photos and shared on their social networking sites right on the spot, checking their profiles to see reactions by others online. Indeed, I sometimes hear older Chinese complain about the ever-increasingly common sight of a group of young adults in restaurants, each one absorbed in the world of their mobile phones rather than interacting with each other.

I asked Gu Hui to speak more about why it was so important to share these experiences in the moment with her online friends. She thought for a minute, and gave another example.

> I went shopping today after work. I went to the Coach store and bought the bag I have been thinking about for a month now. The first thing I did when I got home was log onto my microblog and upload a picture of it. I felt so proud to own it. I like sharing what I buy with others because it's like sharing my happiness. Since having my microblog account, I think I am closer to my friends and we can share our moods anytime and anywhere.

As we continued our conversation and it became clear how much time she spent shuttling back and forth between the virtual and the physical worlds, she gave yet another example of how social sharing, online access, and consumption practices came together for her:

> Last weekend, I was at the store and could not decide between two dresses. I took photos of myself wearing both in the dressing room, and posted them on QQ in a group chat with my two best friends. Within five minutes, both had given me their advice. Luckily, both agreed on the same dress, which gave me more confidence in making the right decision.

These forms of sharing create consumption experiences on multiple levels. Gu Hui and those who post their experiences become informal advertisers among their networks. They also create opportunities for vicarious consumption as they share photos and posts. In the consumption of social media, Chinese consumers imagine themselves in new vignettes of shopping, eating, and experiencing. They engage in a form of group consumption, in which peer groups plan, execute, experience, and share events such as restaurant visits, through the medium of the virtual world while also interacting in the physical world.

Consumers in China are also creating new forms of sociality through their virtu-real contexts. Gu Hui described using QQ to communicate with her colleagues who were just an arm length's away. I heard many others describe similar situations. A teenage girl from Shanghai said:

> After taking a bath in the evening, I went to Taobao again and looked for bags. I chatted with my roommates on QQ in a group about these bags. Maybe it wasn't necessary to chat online as we were in the same room, but it is still troublesome to see those pictures of bags if we all have to share one screen. So we all look on our own computers and share our thoughts in a QQ group – even though we are in the same dorm room!

Even situations in which people can communicate face-to-face become occasions for virtu-real communication, with the online capabilities actually enhancing the shared consumption experience.

The popularity of group purchases, or *tuangou*, reflects the social nature of consumption in China. Seeing a *tuangou* deal on a site like *Dianping* is the perfect excuse to suggest to a group of friends an after work or weekend outing. In fact, it seems that for many young professionals like Gu Hui, organizing after work get-togethers occupies a significant amount of time per day. *Dianping* not only provides users with reviews of places, it actually inspires social consumption through displaying group purchase offers. When a decision is made, all the participants download the necessary coupon onto their phones, and are ready for the evening outing.

Many social commentators have noted that China's youth generation suffers from loneliness due to the fact that they are Singletons, without siblings or cousins. While it is impossible to make such a sweeping generalization, I have found in my own research a strong, almost insatiable desire among young people in China to be with others, whether in the physical or virtual world, and to receive peer validation. Some teens expressed a kind of fear of being alone. In addition, they express some insecurity in navigating consumer spaces on their own. As explored earlier, consumers in China look for mentorship to make up for the fact that their elders have not been able to guide them through these new experiences. They seek out companionship in their consumer journeys. They also seek to share events, whether big or small, in order for the event to feel satisfying. It is almost as if the event was planned just so that it could be shared. Consumer experiences become meaningful once they are socially shared.

THEORETICAL CONSIDERATIONS

New spaces of consumption in China have not just impacted the way people shop but have also created deep sociological shifts. Under Mao, spaces outside the home were monitored by the state and all activities in them subject to critique and censure. Mass rallies, voluntary work, collective parties, and other forms of "organized sociality" in which the state and its agents played a central role dominated the public sphere. City squares, auditoriums, and workers' clubs became sites of state disciplining and, for citizens, spaces where support of the CCP's socialist goals were unquestionable. In order to constantly remind its citizens of what proper revolutionary behavior entailed, socialist slogans and posters depicting revolutionary activities typically covered public walls. These were daily reminders for people to uphold the goals of their socialist society – *Shixian sige xiandaihua*: Achieve the Four Modernisations, *Wei renmin fuwu*: Serve the people, We must grasp revolution and increase production, increase work, increase preparation for struggle, to do an even better job (Yan 2003).

Today, the commercialization of public space has served to trans-
form these spaces, which were once dominated by socialist ideology,
into public celebrations of individual desires, life aspirations, and personal connections. Spaces become sites for the blending of consumption and socializing, as consumers seek to experiment with new
consumer practices within the "safe" environment of peer support.
Within these spaces, individuals, friends and families enact private
moments – reinforcing familial bonds, exploring personal identities,
and seeking pleasure and indulgence. Public spaces have thus increasingly become staging areas for private pleasures and individual desires.
They have become "personalized," in the sense that personal aspirations
and desires can be played out in what was once the domain of enacting
proper political ideology. Consumption spaces are sites where social
relationships become reconstituted through various practices of shopping and identity formation (Miller et al. 1998: 27).

The majority of studies upon which consumption theories have
developed, however, focus on activities in face-to-face, brick-and-
mortar environments. Shopping places are defined in terms of malls,
grocery stores, and other geographically defined environments. As we
explored in this chapter, consumption in China transcends physical
and virtual realms. When the internet is analyzed in relation to consumption, it tends to be framed as secondary to the "real" world of brick
and mortar shopping. Oh and Arditi articulate a common sentiment:

> Cyberstores do not create an experience such as the smell of perfume
> or the feel of silky fabrics that are at hand in malls and department
> stores. Most internet shopping sites promote their advantages strictly
> in terms of convenience and price, not in terms of a call to the senses.
> (2000: 84)

There is a growing set of literature on the internet in China, but its
focus is on the question of its role in an emerging public sphere (see

Hjorth and Arnold, 2012 for one very illuminating exception). The fact that internet search is restricted in terms of politically sensitive topics such as Tibet, and global companies such as Twitter, Facebook, Wikipedia, and YouTube are blocked in China, has facilitated the general consensus that China has yet to develop a true civil society. The absence of such global brands in China also fosters the general impression that China does not have a rich or well-developed internet culture. As we have seen in this chapter, that is not the case, as China's domestic internet companies have created equivalent and, in some cases, functionally superior online solutions.

What I have found is that the effectiveness of the internet has been its use as a way to create rich experiences for its users from both sensory and emotional perspectives. True, people cannot smell and touch objects while online (yet) but they can engage in rich visual sharing and conversations that bring to life their own and others' fantasies around these commodities and other consumer experiences. While the internet in China may be found lacking or flawed by Western commentators from the perspective of a politically "free" public sphere, it has nonetheless played an immense role in the consumer revolution. It has facilitated an inextricable bond between consumption and communication, between acquisition and connectivity. While it has not (yet) played an overtly pivotal role in terms of political revolution (which we will explore more in the chapter on Awareness), it has become the center of China's consumer revolution. Online spaces are as much "cathedrals of consumption" as Apple or Nike stores (Ritzer 2010).

The dynamics of how people move seamlessly between physical and virtual realities call for a reconceptualization of space, recognizing the realities of how people consume across online and offline contexts, without privileging either as more "real" or "authentic." Geographer Doreen Massey offers a direction to follow for a more fluid way of conceptualizing space, which allows for the inclusion of multiple forms.

As she puts it, space is not just the flat land upon which we walk, but also a dimension of multiplicity. Space, in this more conceptual form, is made up of our relations and connections with each other, which are, of course, fraught with inequality and power differentials (2005). Following Massey's suggestion, we can frame the intersections between the virtual and the physical as a social space, within which consumer connections are expressed, fostered, harnessed, and exploited. As consumers develop new paths through these emerging spaces, they create different forms of social dynamics and desire fulfillment.

Building on Massey's framework, this chapter suggests the concept of the "virtu-real" as a way of reflecting the realities of consumption practices in China today. This way of framing the contexts of consumer activities acknowledges the seamlessness with which people are increasingly moving between the physical world and the internet world. Perhaps more importantly, what we see in China is that people often inhabit both worlds at the same time, layering the experiences of one on top of the other. For an increasing number of young consumers, in particular, consumption experiences are not complete without the flexible experience of moving between virtual and physical. This ability to consume, commune, and communicate in the virtu-real does not merely indicate more transactional options, but also reflects the emotional and social aspects of these shared experiences. Access to the internet via mobile devices, the proliferation of social networking sites, the ability to share video and photos as well as one's thoughts – all contribute to the phenomenon that consumers in China are never more than just a click away from the marketplace.

3 | Status ———————————

When we met in 2012, Da Shan was a 36-year-old entrepreneur. He ran an internet startup in Shanghai, and was hopeful that the idea would become the next big thing among tech enthusiasts. He was, by all accounts, successful and well off, with a monthly income of 20,000 yuan, compared to the monthly average of about 5,000 yuan for professional workers. He and his wife lived in an upscale, newly constructed apartment complex in a suburb of Shanghai, which, he was proud to say, had its own supermarket, gym, and kindergarten. He traveled when he could and was hoping to buy a Land Rover SUV because it "represents the spirit of adventure." When I asked him to elaborate on what it was like to be a successful entrepreneur, he turned the conversation to the broader historical context:

> In the last 30 years, the biggest change is that we no longer "eat from the same big pot." In the past, our work was more or less the same, the aim was to pursue stability. The iron rice bowl was guaranteed for our whole lives. No matter what your ability was or how enthusiastically you worked before, you would gain no career development or material rewards because in that crazy era, you were born with your status and your class consciousness. But the last 30 years have brought enormous changes. In the 1980s the reforms have changed everyone's views of social status. During that first decade, a small number of brave and diligent people were able to get wealthy, but there were still a lot of structural barriers that prevented most people from achieving material

prosperity. In the 1990s, more and more people were able to adapt to changes. As we step into the twenty-first century, the access to information and foreign cultures is changing people's ideas. We now believe we can use our own intellect, science, and technology to change our lives, enjoy all kinds of services, and experience new things. For example, my university major was mechanics. Based on that, I should have been assigned to work in a factory, doing the same repetitive work every day. But instead, I can pursue my own plans for my future life and I want to use my mind and hands to change something. Today's social environment allows you to make your own decisions. I have chosen to start my own business. My parents could not have imagined such a thing for themselves.

When Mao Zedong and the Chinese Communist Party came to power in 1949, they proclaimed the existence of only three social strata: workers, peasants, and a small intellectual class that would, according to Marxist theory, gradually shrink. The "exploitative classes" of pre-revolutionary time – the landowners, capitalists, and factory owners – were to be stripped of their power and resources, with the ultimate goal of establishing a classless society. Such calls to action intensified during the Cultural Revolution, when Mao Zedong called on the masses to struggle against the exploitative classes. The three decades of rule under Mao Zedong created a redistribution system based on a planned economy that prevented people from amassing wealth and capital through the free market, erasing at least the outward appearances of class inequality. In 1978, Deng Xiaoping abandoned the notion of class struggle as the center of his political strategy, focusing instead on market reforms to restart a stagnant economy. His policies around gradually privatizing the economy paved the way for the re-emergence of inequality based on wealth in China.

In explaining his own success story, Da Shan described the "iron rice bowl." This idiom refers to the system of guaranteed lifetime employment in state enterprises under Mao Zedong's regime. Within this system, job security and wages were not related to job performance, but rather, determined by one's adherence to party doctrine. All Chinese workers were under state control, and necessities including housing, food, and clothing rations, as well as permits to change jobs, enter university, travel, marry, and even bear children, were issued by government officials. As Da Shan goes on to say in his narrative, the iron rice bowl did not reward hard work or individual ability. His current success is the result of changes that have opened up the possibility for people to make their own futures – not to be locked in by the "class consciousness" they were born with or other constraints such as educational background.

The smashing of the iron rice bowl and Deng Xiaoping's exhortation that "to get rich is glorious" have led to the fierce re-emergence of social distinction practices in China. The lifestyles of Shanghai's new rich, with their European sports cars, luxury high-rise apartments, and shopping vacations to Beverly Hills, stand in stark contrast to the living conditions of the urban poor. The latter includes migrants from rural areas, who live several to a dorm room and work long hours in factories producing commodities such as iPhones and Nike shoes. While propaganda posters exhorting citizens to expose the counter-revolutionary classes once lined city centers, today, large advertisements featuring models in expensive clothing and brandishing luxury products appeal to those passing by. In 2013, the number of billionaires in China exceeded 300, putting it second only to the USA in terms of total number (*Business Insider* 2013).

This chapter explores emerging forms of social status in China. How are they expressed, and what role does consumption play?

CONSPICUOUS CONSUMPTION

In China, we see incredible social mobility, unparalleled in any other time in the country's history as well as any other place in the world. In the context of such mobility, the ownership, use, and display of consumer goods communicate one's social status. In *The Theory of the Leisure Class*, Thorstein Veblen argued that in modern society, wealth, rather than military prowess, had become the basis of social status. Yet it was not always obvious how much wealth people had. Thus, the display of objects and the air of an idle lifestyle became the primary means of communicating status. Veblen coined the term "conspicuous consumption" to indicate that consumption acts were not just about fulfilling individual needs and desires, but about communicating to others one's place in the social hierarchy (1899).

The term "conspicuous consumption" is a term I hear often in reference to consumer behaviors in China. What is significant is not just the sheer size of the luxury goods market, but the fact that despite their lower average household incomes, consumers in China are purchasing more high-end products than their counterparts in the majority of developed nations. Owning prestige brands when it comes to fashion, accessories, autos, and technology appears to be a national obsession. And while middle-income consumers cannot afford everything they desire, they do attempt to purchase a few, highly visible luxury items in order to demonstrate their participation in China's consumer culture.

Forms of conspicuous consumption do not remain static, however. These changes are reflected in the common Chinese phrase, the "three must haves," which describe the most popular commodities that bestow social status. In the 1980s, as the country was just emerging from the most ideologically driven period of time under the Cultural Revolution, the three must haves included a bicycle, a watch, and a sewing machine. By the 1990s, the must haves included a refrigerator, TV, and air conditioner. When I first lived in China in 1990, I recall my surprise at seeing refrigerators in people's living rooms. They were not tucked away in a corner, but rather, placed so that they were prominently displayed – almost like shrines. Because people do not have the habit of socializing in Chinese kitchens, there would have been no way that guests could have seen the refrigerator had it been in the kitchen. Instead, consumers back then understood the symbolic power of placing their precious new commodities in what sociologist Goffman would call the front stages of their home (1959). The refrigerator, placed in a visible and central location in this front stage, signified the family's upward mobility and also their knowledge of what was worthy of owning. Newly purchased televisions were often covered with doilies or other decorative covers, drawing attention to their preciousness.

During the early twenty-first century, the must haves moved into high tech. I began to see PCs in the living rooms as well, also taking up space in central parts of the most "front stage" areas of the home. Mobile phones became highly visible prestige items that both adorned the body and signified the vitality of one's social networks. Being adept at the internet also became a form of conspicuous consumption, as netizens began to make online reputations for themselves through building their social media following, posting photos and reviews about their own consumption experiences, and accumulating social capital in the virtual world.

The desire to acquire and conspicuously consume luxury products has led to some interesting behaviors in China. In the 1990s and early 2000s, it was not uncommon to see Chinese men leave the label sewn to the sleeve – this allowed others to see what brands they were wearing. In my home ethnographies, I often observed that luxury cosmetics were left in their original packaging and displayed prominently on desks or dresser tops. When wine was first introduced into China, businessmen who hoped to impress their colleagues or clients would often buy expensive bottles and then gulp them down like shots of hard liquor. Even if someone cannot afford a luxury item, there are other ways they associate themselves with the brand. Purchasing smaller, branded items, such as a Coach wallet, instead of a handbag, or carrying a branded shopping bag, allows people to participate in a kind of conspicuous brand consumption at a lower price point. And as I noted earlier, consumers in China like to save branded shopping bags and reuse them, even if it is to carry a homemade lunch, to make it appear as if they have been shopping.

By 2010, the must have items were significantly more expensive than in earlier decades. Owning a car had become one of the most important forms of conspicuous consumption, reflected in the fact that China has surpassed the USA as the biggest market for new car sales in the world (Branigan 2012). Feng Sha Chen, a wealthy female executive, described her own journey to success through her car ownership:

> I bought my first car in 1995. I was still single then. At that time in China, the days you could drive depended on whether your license plate had an odd or even number at the end. I bought one that allowed me to drive every day, which cost a lot – almost two-thirds the price of the car itself. But the fact that I could do this spoke for my personal capabilities and allowed me to stand out from the majority.

I asked her to talk about her current car, and what it said about her.

> I now own a BMW X3 red sports cars. She has a strong appearance and a surging heart. Her outstanding performance satisfies my mature self, enabling me to feel full of passion when I drive her. The car also represents my attitude and reflects my quality of life.

Chris Liu, a market-research consultant based in Shanghai, stressed that all of the social pressure to own the must haves could become daunting. "To find a wife, you need a car and a house. Without these things, you won't get a second look." Chris eventually did buy a car and a house, and not long after, he found a wife, but his lament reflects the pressures and expectations of China's youth generation when it comes to conspicuous consumption and finding life partners. Such tensions were reflected in the media storm surrounding the responses of a particular contestant on the dating reality show "*Fei Cheng Wu Rao*" (literally meaning "don't disturb me if you are not sincere"). The reality show features single women lining up on stage to judge potential suitors. One by one, male candidates introduce themselves and answer questions. The women press a button to turn off the light in front of them if they have no interest in him. In a now famous incident, one young woman responded to a suitor's offer to take her for a ride on his bike with: "I'd rather cry in a BMW car than laugh on the back seat of a bicycle." This response set the social media world on fire, as netizens either scorned the young woman for portraying the post-1980s generation as overly materialistic, or applauded her for speaking the truth about the youth generation's desire for status items.

Those international corporations that have been most successful in China have capitalized on the fact that Chinese consumers are not necessarily following the same behaviors as the developed markets a few decades back. Their habits and practices around conspicuous consumption are shaped by their own specific contexts, and they assign different meanings and bring varying expectations to their consumer choices. Companies, thus, have had to localize their offerings. For example, luxury cars in China are often driven by a chauffeur, as opposed to the car owner. Automakers have modified luxury models to suit China's new rich by designing bigger back seats, which have become the focal point of the cars. High-end cosmetics brands from Europe and the United States have altered their offerings for China. Based on the insight that beauty in China is strongly correlated with pale skin, cosmetics companies have created skin-whitening products to appeal to the expectations of female consumers. Western fast-food restaurants such as McDonald's and KFC offer localized menus, featuring some Chinese-inspired dishes like Peking duck wrap, red bean ice-cream, and taro pie. Pizza Hut has tapped into Chinese desires for conspicuous consumptions by refashioning itself as a more upscale dining establishment than it is in the USA. Unlike in the USA, where

Pizza Hut restaurants resemble fast-food restaurants, in China, the place is a desired destination for families, who enjoy the ambiance as much as, or even more than, the food itself.

LUXURY GOODS

Xiao Xiao is the 54-year-old retiree we met in an earlier chapter, who reminisced about the joy of the four cent popsicle during her childhood. When we met, she was single and lived alone in a complex with other retirees. While she lived fairly modestly in a small apartment and dressed plainly, I soon discovered that she loved collecting designer goods, and had a collection of Hermes scarves still in their original packaging, tucked away in her closet. I asked her where she bought her stuff.

> My friends and I go on a couple of trips together every year. Our favorite destination is Hong Kong, because we can go shopping for luxury items. We buy famous bags and leather belts as well as cosmetics.

I asked her if they go sightseeing on these trips, and she continues:

> Only the first time. After that, it's boring to go to the same sites again. We prefer to spend our time shopping for high-end goods. That's what we go there to do.

In 2012, Chinese shoppers surpassed those from the USA to become the world's top spenders on luxury goods. Chinese shoppers represent one fourth of the total global spending on such high ticket items from top notch brands. In just the past decade, China has become the biggest market for such established, global prestige brands as Louis Vuitton, Chanel, and Gucci (D'Arpizio 2012).

Corporate marketers and consumer researchers new to China are typically shocked when they find out who China's luxury consumers are. As in other countries, a portion of luxury goods are purchased by the ultra-rich – China's millionaires and billionaires. However, the bulk of luxury goods are purchased not by the economic elite, but rather, by those with fairly average urban professional incomes. These tend to be middle-income professionals who splurge on a few luxury items every year – but there are enough of these en masse to help create the world's largest luxury market. A second fact that surprises most is the relative youth of these shoppers, who are between 25 and 28 years old, a good 15 years younger than similar consumers from Europe, and 25 years younger than those from the USA. The typical profile of the luxury brand shopper is an unmarried young adult, still living at home with his or her parents. While their incomes are not especially high, they have no expenses as they are expected to live at home until they get married. In addition to being able to spend their own salaries any way they like, as Singletons, they are the sole recipient of any discretionary income from their parents and grandparents. Thus, while wealthy political elite and business owners certainly buy luxury goods, it is these younger, middle-income shoppers who are shaping the market for global high-end brands.

Renee Hartmann, co-founder of consulting group China Luxury Advisors, says that international luxury brands have taken notice of China's younger demographic, and have altered their strategies to continue their appeal with this market. Brands such as Coach, Burberry, and Dionne Van Fusberg have started aggressive social media campaigns, understanding that Chinese consumers create strong word of mouth through online reviews and microblogging. They have also started offering more affordable products, such as Coach wallets, to appeal to Chinese consumers who want to be associated with the brand but cannot afford a full blown Coach bag just yet. As Hartmann advises her clients, these brands realize that if they capture the loyalties of these segments early, they will retain them as they move up the economic ladder and can afford higher ticket items.

According to a study by McKinsey & Company, Chinese consumer familiarity with luxury goods has grown tremendously. By 2010, they were familiar with nearly twice as many brands as they were in 2008 (Atsmon et al. 2012). As we explored in the chapter on Spaces, urban centers have transformed from dreary state-run shopping experiences to neon cathedrals of consumption, where luxury items are displayed in branded stores, inviting shoppers into the fantasy of the lifestyles they symbolize. Advertisements have replaced socialist slogans, and also serve to entice as well as educate consumers as to the desirability of brands. Luxury brands worn by stars in such popular shows as *Gossip Girl* also create interest and demand.

But perhaps most importantly, people are learning about luxury brands through the internet. There are also more websites dedicated to luxury items, such as Affinity China, which is a private social network that offers news about luxury lifestyle and travel opportunities. Affinity China features blogs about topics such as travel destinations with VIP packages, high priced real estate in places such as Southern California, Paris Fashion Week, and private viewings of exclusive jewelry collections. In one entry, readers are given a glimpse of a VIP shopping tour itinerary on the West Coast of the USA over the Chinese New Year holiday, which includes shopping at stores featuring Louis Vuitton, Dior, Hermes, and Gucci.

While the number of stores carrying luxury goods has expanded dramatically over the last two decades, consumers prefer buying luxury goods while on vacation outside China. The average Chinese tourist in France, for example, spends roughly $1,900 on shopping, far more than any other tourists (Boehler 2012). International shopping destinations may include nearby destinations such as Hong Kong and Singapore, or further away destinations such as Dubai and Los Angeles. There are several reasons why they prefer to buy their luxury goods abroad, even if they are available domestically. The first is that luxury items carry a heavy tax in China, rendering some items up to 60 percent more expensive domestically than abroad. The second reason is authenticity. Purchasing products abroad ensures that they are not knock-offs. The third reason is uniqueness – shopping abroad gives them more opportunities to purchase something not available in China, and yet still clearly prestigious because of its brand association.

China's luxury shoppers are looking not only for branded products, but also for luxury or unique experiences. As we explore further in the chapter on Commodification, residential areas mimicking British or French towns are hoping to fulfill the fantasies of aspiring home owners to live a foreign lifestyle. Consumers are increasingly expecting VIP treatment when they shop for luxury goods, including champagne, private fashion shows, and a sense of exclusivity. French-style chateaus are being built in the countryside to attract visitors to a nascent wine industry.

While marketers tend to associate China with conspicuous consumption of "blingy" luxury items, in recent years, luxury consumers have transitioned to more subtle forms. Patricia Pao conducted one of the very first surveys with China's billionaires. In 2009, she interviewed 353 of them on their tastes and brand preferences, providing marketers a unique look into their lifestyles. She has repeated the study every year since then, and notes that these elite consumers are moving away from "bling" and towards more understated, but still luxurious brands. As an example, she says Prada and Hermes have become more popular in recent years, due to their subtle branding, while Louis Vuitton and Burberry have become known for being too obvious and symbolic of people who are "trying too hard to make a statement."

According to Renee Hartmann, co-founder of the consultancy, China Luxury Advisors, there are two kinds of ultra-rich in China. The first is what Hartmann calls the "internationalized wealthy first-tier rich." These consumers typically speak some English, and have often studied or worked abroad. The second type is the "local wealthy" – those from second or other lower tier cities. They are more locally based, less international in their experiences. The former typically live in the coastal cities such as Shanghai and Guangzhou, regularly travel abroad, and may have lived abroad for some time. Their tastes are thus heavily influenced by those cosmopolitan experiences. The local luxury classes include entrepreneurs who may run state-owned or partially state-owned enterprises in the second and third-tier cities. They tend to have less international experience, but develop their tastes through the Chinese media, as well as through observing their peers in the first-tier cities.

Pao believes that one of the key reasons for this shift towards less showy brands is the desire for the ultra-rich to demonstrate their status, given that even middle-income consumers and the local luxury class from smaller cities are emulating their tastes by purchasing luxury items.

> The newly minted billionaires want to stand out, they don't want to carry what others are carrying.

Kelvin Ma, Managing Director of Oracle Added Value, a brand strategy firm in Shanghai, observes that first-tier city consumers are similarly trying to differentiate themselves from the upcoming second, third and fourth-tier city consumers. "The people from the first-tier cities want to differentiate themselves from what they think are the less sophisticated people of smaller cities. But when the people from smaller cities buy the same luxury items, what can they do? They move on to champion new brands to continually stay ahead." This desire to stay ahead of the pack is also a prime driver for purchasing luxury items abroad, on the chance of scoring unique, limited edition items that are not available to the ordinary shopper.

Another emerging behavior is the growing acceptance, at least in China's first-tier cities, of secondhand luxury items. Stores selling very lightly used items such as luxury handbags are gaining popularity, especially among the young, upwardly mobile consumers who are not the economically elite but aspire to own a piece of luxury for themselves. The stigma of secondhand is still strong, but as consumers travel more they see that used luxury items are also being sold in places such as Tokyo and Hong Kong.

Counterfeit goods also play a role in the ecosystem of luxury shopping. China is notorious for copying everything from Louis Vuitton handbags to Rolex watches to iPhones. In most major cities, there are areas of town known for selling "knock-offs." Western governments have criticized China for such violations of intellectual property rights. Nonetheless, this seems to have done little to dampen the activities of the copycat industry. Pirated goods can easily be found in privately owned stores. There was even a spotting of a copycat Apple store selling fake Apple products, such as the HiPhone. Such counterfeit goods have become global products in their own right. They are shipped to destinations such as Brazil, where they are sold in downtown Sao Paulo.

While pirated goods serve a purpose in that they allow consumers to, as Jessica Lin argues, "seek the symbolism of the brand without having to pay the cost," they are gradually losing their appeal among consumers in China who want to build their status (2011: 3). As Chinese consumers become more savvy about the visual differences between authentic and fake products, they become worried that counterfeit products will reflect badly on them. "I don't want to be thought of as a miserly person!" said Zheng Zheng, a 23-year-old woman in Shanghai who works in retail. She would rather wait to buy the real thing than have the fake version today. People want others to know they have the real thing, but they increasingly also want the self-satisfaction that can only come from the sense of authenticity. To be caught with a fake would be to admit that one is only interested in the conspicuousness of display, and that one is not truly successful. As such, consumers in China go to great lengths to prove something is authentic, especially if it is a gift. The best method is buying it abroad from a bona fide branded store, and to make sure the product stays in its original packaging.

Up until very recently, luxury brands always meant foreign brands: European and American brands for fashion and Japanese brands for technology and cosmetics. These countries of origin stand for modern consumer lifestyles and have, for the past few decades, inspired Chinese imaginations about their own futures. While there is still no truly global luxury brand that has emerged out of China, the tide is slowly turning.

In March of 2013, Peng Liyuan, wife of the new Chinese president Xi Jinping, became a surprise style sensation on her first official state visit. Stepping off the plane in Moscow, she wore a sophisticated black double-breasted belted coat and elegant handbag, with her hair neatly pinned up. The fact that China finally had a first lady who looked well put together was a sensation in itself. However, what took the Chinese public by storm was the fact that she chose a home-grown, domestic fashion brand. The private fashion brand, Exception, is based out of Guangzhou, and has been described as one of China's leading independent labels. As their website says, the designers strive for simple and unique designs that do not copy Western brands, but seek a distinctly domestic style while appealing to the new, cosmopolitan Chinese woman. The label has expanded, with nearly 100 stores and retail counters in China. Style watchers immediately anointed her the "Michelle Obama" of China, as the US First Lady has also been known to draw attention to unknown, domestic designers. Ever since she debuted the look, online searches for everything she has worn have ignited a newfound fascination with Chinese fashion brands. The interest even crashed Exception's website the day after the photos of the first lady went viral.

Shang Xia represents another potential player in the race for a truly global Chinese luxury brand. *Shang Xia*, which means Up Down in Mandarin, is a collaboration between the Hermes Group and Jiang Qiong Er, a Chinese artist and the company's CEO. It opened its doors in 2010 on Shanghai's Huaihai Road, and showcases an exquisite collection of handcrafted jewelry, furniture, clothing, porcelain, and home decorations. Although connected to the Hermes brand, *Shang Xia* is positioned as an exclusively Chinese lifestyle brand, which takes its inspiration from China's tradition of fine craftsmanship. As stated on its website, it "is a brand for art of living that promises a unique encounter with the heritage of Chinese design and craftsmanship . . . *Shang Xia* has the ambition to preserve the beauty and techniques of traditional craftsmanship and embrace the elegance and simplicity of a new twenty-first-century aesthetic."

While it is still unclear whether consumers in China will embrace *Shang Xia* as a luxury brand, the case with the fashion brand Exception demonstrates the influence China's celebrities can have in creating widespread interest in domestic brands. Up until very recently, Chinese consumers primarily embraced brands that had been established outside China, looking to what consumers abroad were doing for their consumption cues. There are growing numbers of signs that they are starting to look at China's own, home-grown talent for inspiration on what the next status items will be.

MIDDLE-CLASS CONSCIOUSNESS

While the numbers around China's ultra-rich have certainly caught the attention of companies offering luxury products and experiences, it is in fact China's middle class that has elicited the most attention from both academic and business analysts. The interest stems from the general consensus that China's middle class is growing quickly and will eventually make up the largest portion of China's consumer market. Related to that, there is also a preoccupation, especially within the

Western press and observers of China, with the question of whether China will develop a prospering, healthy middle class, which is associated with a stable, thriving economic and political system.

Despite the intense interest in China's middle class, there is no widespread consensus on what "middle class" actually means in this context. Issues such as how big China's middle class is, how much they make, what their lifestyles are like, or even whether the term middle class is appropriate for the Chinese market are open for debate and disagreement. A strictly economic or objectivist approach defines middle class in terms of household income. In these terms, figures for annual income range from US$10,000 to US$60,000 a year. A more subjectivist approach also considers occupation, ownership of certain commodities such as a house and a car, and lifestyle (see Weber 2005 for interaction of economic wealth, social status, and professional prestige in modern societies). Estimates of the size of China's middle class range anywhere from 5 percent to 25 percent of the population. The most optimistic predict that by 2030, 70 percent of the population will reach the middle class (Li 2010).

In addition to the difficulties in defining the middle class, it is also difficult to compare China's middle class with those in other advanced economies. In a country with such vast regional differences, average incomes as well as the lifestyles that these incomes can buy differ significantly among the first, second, third, and fourth-tier cities. The income disparity between urban and rural residents itself is so great that national averages can become meaningless. Furthermore, incomes in China can also be a challenge to measure accurately. Chinese New Year bonuses, which can boost income levels significantly, are typically not reported for tax purposes. It is also difficult to compare lifestyles of people with similar incomes in China and in other developed countries. The practice of living at home until one is married means that adults even into their thirties and forties do not have the same kinds of financial burdens that their peers in the USA may have. Furthermore, as we have discussed throughout this book, China's one-child policy has had a dramatic impact on spend per child, with Singletons receiving all the affection and economic spoilage their parents and grandparents can offer.

My goal is not to try to solve the question of how to define China's middle class objectively and how big it is. There are plenty of sociological studies that can offer quantitatively validated data about who belongs to China's middle class, and who does not. Undoubtedly, the term middle class is and will continue to remain an important socio-economic category for those in academia and business to use, if nothing more than as a short-hand way of describing a certain category of people. However, what I would like to do with this section is focus on the perspectives of Chinese consumers themselves: How do they experience social distinction? Do they talk about it in terms of class, or in different terms? My approach borrows heavily from Mark Liechty, who explored the meanings around middle classness in Nepal. "When writing about class, one has two basic options: either treat 'class' as a given – a taken for granted, natural, universal category or concept that speaks for itself – or attempt actually to explain the word by describing the experience of class in everyday life. It is the latter option, the effort to understand class as cultural life, that poses a challenge to anthropology" (2003: 8). He continues, "The middle class is a constantly renegotiated cultural space – a space of ideas, values, goods, practices and embodied behaviors – in which the terms of inclusion and exclusion are endlessly tested, negotiated, and affirmed. From this point of view, it is the process, not the product, that constitutes class" (2003: 15). Following Liecthy, this section explores the actual experience of social distinction, as opposed to assuming class as a pre-existing category.

What I have found among consumers in China is that, like the literature on class, they too have inconsistent perceptions of what middle class means. Below is a sampling of responses I received in a survey asking people to describe what it means to be middle class:

The household's annual income is over 300,000 yuan. They're usually the middle-level managerial staff in the companies, and are accountants, lawyers, scientific and IT workers, or professionals engaged in art. They can afford their own homes, cars, high quality household electric appliances, art collections, and some luxury goods.

In contrast with the above, this next definition is more modest both in terms of the kinds of professions they can hold as well as the lifestyles they lead.

All ordinary people can be called middle class. They work in various places ranging from offices to factories to the countryside. During their leisure time, they shop, go to the supermarket or vegetable market for food, clothing and other daily supplies. Sometimes they have tea, see movies, or go shopping. Once in a while they go to the spa with their friends.

Others emphasize experiences as opposed to material possessions.

The middle class continually pursues a higher quality of life. People with such lifestyles value things that have culture more than things that simply cost a lot. They pay attention to art, they give to charities, they travel. They like to keep learning new things.

The discussion of class with consumers in China reveals not only a broad range of interpretations, but also a general reticence to define their social worlds by class. This reticence is at least partially due to the still very recent history of class struggle instituted by the CCP under Mao Zedong. Being identified with any class other than the peasant and working-class masses subjected one to public humiliation, re-education camp, and other forms of punishment. Class affiliations can carry negative connotations around what was inherited rather than earned.

But more importantly, people express a discomfort with the fixed, static nature of class. They hesitate to define themselves as settled into a particular socio-economic position. Even when people fit the mid to higher-income levels that are generally considered middle class, I found that they do not naturally think of themselves in such terms. In some cases this was due to their own perception that the middle class is more akin to what would be considered the upper or upper middle class in other developed markets (Li 2010).

Da Shan, whose description of success we explored earlier, did not think of himself as living a middle-class lifestyle, despite the fact that his income was significantly higher than the average urban professional. Instead, he preferred to talk about himself in terms of someone who is still striving and working hard to reach his goals.

> Strictly speaking, there aren't many people who can obtain the middle-class lifestyle in China. These people usually have a house worth two million yuan. They can buy everything with cash, they don't need loans. Even if they do, the payment only takes up 10 percent of their monthly income. They have a private car worth 250,000 yuan. They have savings in the bank and invest in stocks. They take long vacations twice a year. One person in the couple might be the senior executive in a company and the other might be an entrepreneur. They don't pay much attention to the price when making purchases. They spend a certain proportion of their money on health including body-building, body care or health products. On weekends they hold family parties to enjoy life. I'm still working hard in my career so work is most important. I still have a big distance and gap before touching this kind of lifestyle.

In recent years, there has also been a growing disdain for people who flaunt their wealth, and in particular, those whose wealth is due to their political connections. The distaste for politicians who distinguish themselves through conspicuous consumption is in no small part related to the cases of corruption that have been highlighted in the Chinese media. The past five years have seen the investigation of several high-level officials including former party boss Bo Xilai, who was once considered the front runner for the top post in China's leadership. Numerous cases of party bosses misusing funds to support their extravagant lifestyles have fostered a deep sense of distrust among the public. Despite heavy state control over content, social media and blogs have allowed people to express their frustration over the wealthy elite and out of touch politicians. As one 30-year-old male who worked in HR put it:

> The luxury lifestyle in China is associated with corruption. People who go to those really expensive high-end clubs are going to parties where they bribe officials. I don't have any good impressions about them. I don't want to get close to this kind of lifestyle.

The message of frustration with China's elite has not gone unheeded. Much was made in social media and the press over the attendants of the National People's Congress in early 2013, which included 83 billionaires. Compared to years past, in which this political meeting looked more like a Hollywood red carpet event, delegates toned down their conspicuous consumption by driving less ostentatious cars and wearing more modest suits and jewelry. Even China's leader, Xi Jinping, has spoken out against the unnecessary flaunting of wealth, in an attempt to dampen public anger over corruption and social inequality.

The public disdain also extends to the ostentatious spending habits of those who inherited their wealth, typically through the political connections of their parents. Feng Sha Chen, a female executive who, like Da Shan, achieved her own success through hard work, had some harsh words to say about the so-called princelings, or children of rich party officials.

People like the rich second generation of officials have nothing to do but drive sports cars around or spend millions of dollars on shopping trips. It's a world of difference between their lives and ours. They have airplanes, limited edition cars, and villas in scenic areas. They eat and get together in places which ordinary people hardly go to. They isolate themselves from the outside world and don't associate with ordinary people. They pack their lives with luxury goods, but do not understand that a true luxury lifestyle does not have to be made up of expensive ornaments, precious jewelry, extravagant leather goods, or famous watches. They are not interesting people to me.

Feng Sha Chen's comments reflect the sentiments I have heard among many individuals in China who are, by objective measures, doing very well for themselves financially. Rather than seeking to emulate the ultra-rich, or at least those ultra-rich whose lifestyles were not earned, they prefer to distance themselves. While the notion of class based on objective measures such as income and product ownership continues to be a significant framing concept in both the academic and business literature on China, it is nonetheless important to also explore its limitations. In the case of people living a so-called middle-class lifestyle in China, there is not a strong sense of class affiliation, but rather, a desire to define themselves through their own, self-earned economic mobility. Furthermore, these middle-income consumers are wary of emulation. They do not try to emulate the ultra-rich, and instead question the latter's motives. While using the term "middle class" to refer to Chinese consumers in a particular income bracket with a certain amount of spending power is convenient, the forms of social distinction that the Chinese themselves gravitate towards are evolving along different lines.

UPWARD MOBILITY

According to Thorstein Veblen, conspicuous consumption entailed not just the display of luxury items, but also the display of a leisurely lifestyle (1899). In the context of his writing, which was the turn-of-the-century USA, being independently wealthy was considered an important social distinguisher. Thus, in striving to build status, people displayed not only what they could afford to buy but also the lifestyle of being idle and not having to get involved in the unsavory business of making money. Veblen observed that those who had to work to make a living nonetheless strove to give off the impression of idleness, through participating in country clubs and the like. He called this "conspicuous leisure." His interrelated concepts reflect a particular social and historical context, in which being idle and wealthy was the most desirable status.

The situation differs in China, however. The desire to display one's wealth through the acquisition, ownership, and use of prestige items is certainly common, and forms the basis of what most analysts and marketers mean when they refer to conspicuous consumption in China. However, unlike Veblen's subjects in turn-of-the-century USA, consumers in China seek to display their hard work, entrepreneurialism, and potential for upward mobility. Being idle or not having "earned" one's wealth has strong negative connotations among the so-called middle class. Veblen's turn-of-the-century Europeans would have found Chinese consumer practices when it comes to conspicuous consumption distasteful.

Consumers themselves frame status in terms of one's own personal ability to create opportunities. People who demonstrate more upward mobility – the ability to nurture, create, and realize their own success – are perceived as having higher status. In this sense, social distinction is not so much about markers of "having made it" but rather, markers of "moving on up." I first noticed the emphasis on self-made success in my research on lifestyles among the well-to-do in China. One of the questions I posed to all of the participants in this study was how they would describe their ideal day and their ideal lifestyle. Not surprisingly, most answers included references to consumption activities, such as going to the spa or going shopping. However, what I did not expect was the equal, if not greater, emphasis people placed on work as an important part of the ideal way to live. Jiang Hu Diao was a 25-year-old owner of a popular hot-pot restaurant near a university. This excerpt from his journal reflects the common sentiment that work is as important as consumption in people's aspirational lifestyles.

My ideal life includes owning an apartment and a car and having a happy family. I want to have a work situation that allows me to express my true abilities. An ideal day would include having breakfast with my family in the morning, sending the kid to school and my wife to work, and then going to work myself. At work, my ideal situation is to have a staff that communicates well with me. I imagine having a happy lunch with the staff, sometimes treating them to food and discussing business at the tea house. After work, I pick up my wife and kid, and cook for them, and help my kid with homework. And then end the day with a beer.

When I asked Jiang Hu Diao who embodied the characteristics that he admired, instead of naming someone in his own life, he named Li Kaifu. Li Kaifu was the founding president of Google China, and currently authors a personal website to coach young people in their careers.

Li Kaifu cares about young people. His blog is about coaching us to start our own businesses. His ideas have had a strong impact on me. He said you should face the idea of starting a business with vision and confidence, assess your own skills, and go in with a clear mind and vision. His words have helped to shape my own career.

The importance of demonstrating one's accomplishment through work, and not just wealth, connects consumption to production within Chinese perceptions of social status. This is significant in light of the often artificial distinction between production and consumption within the body of consumption work. Marx's work on commodity fetishism and alienation addressed the experiences of the consumer, but his focus was in fact people's roles at work, whether they were at the top of the hierarchy or the exploited workers. Early consumption theory, influenced by Marx, continued to privilege production as a focus. More recent work, influenced by postmodern theory, has seen the shift towards the perspective of consumers as active, self-aware agents who, through their acquisition and use of products, experiment with subjectivities and social distinctions. However, some have argued that each perspective on its own artificially separates people's consumer behaviors from their money-making activities.

Among consumers in China, we witness this inextricable dynamic – in consuming, people seek to express something about their own self-made accomplishments. There is no attempt to hide hard work or the fact that one has come from a difficult or humble background. In fact, such narratives of upward mobility and entrepreneurialism are valued over the appearance of idleness. Feeling satisfied as a consumer is linked to feeling fulfilled as a producer.

GUANXI AND MOBILE PHONES

In academic studies about Chinese social status and business success, the concept of *guanxi* emerges frequently. *Guanxi*, or personal networks, are based on the cultivation of relationships and networks of mutual dependence. They require the manufacturing of obligation and indebtedness through the exchange of gifts and favors. Participants in webs of *guanxi* are implicitly obliged to give, to receive, and to repay. Individuals with good reputations in various webs of *guanxi* acquire leverage that can be used in other interactions. In the post-Mao era of economic liberalization, personal networks have become one of the primary means by which individuals navigate the disjunctures and radical shifts in China's social order. *Guanxi* thus represents a form of social capital. The more connections one has, the more accomplished one appears to be (Yang 1994).

Building *guanxi* is not a new practice in China. Even under Mao Zedong's rule, when the playing field for all was supposedly leveled, people with connections to party officials had more access to scarce goods via unofficial black market channels. New venues and modes of *guanxi* building, however, have emerged since economic reforms were implemented. Innovations in communication technologies, in particular, have had a tremendous effect on the way *guanxi* is maintained and built.

In the last decade alone, China has leapfrogged from a nation where only a minority of people had landline phones to one where the majority of people have mobile phones. In 2012, the number of mobile phone users in China hit one billion (Flannery 2012). The variety of models available, from high-end iPhones and Samsung Galaxy smartphones, to lower end domestic brands, have made it possible for nearly 70 percent of the population to own a mobile device.

In my own research on mobile phones in China for technology companies, I have observed some unique behaviors around phones as status objects. The first, which most Westerners observe right away, is the very conspicuous way in which mobile phones are used and handled. Much more so than in the USA, phones are thought of as fashion accessories, items that adorn the body. When I first began doing research on mobile phones in the early 2000s, I was struck by the gendered nature of phones – there were heart-bejeweled, heart-shaped phones for women, dark and sharp-edged phones for men. The women I interviewed talked about the importance of the phone looking good next to their faces, and reflecting the slim look they desired for themselves. Men wanted phones that looked professional when worn on their belt buckle, giving them the appearance of authority. Such differences in technology as a form of adornment reflected the increasing freedom people felt to express gender identities (Sugiyama 2009). By 2012, industrial designs are less obviously gendered, but there is still the strong sense that a phone is not just a tool but a reflection of self.

"If cost is not a consideration, I want to have something in the Samsung I9220 series. I saw it used in a Korean drama by one of my favorite actresses. Both the phone and the actress looked so good," said a female retail worker in Shanghai.

The brand of one's mobile phone, like other luxury or high-end commodities, also reflects consumers' desires to portray themselves as modern. Zhu Long, the Apple enthusiast we met in the chapter on Spaces, said: "Apple represents science and technology innovation. By using an iPhone, I say to others that I am keeping pace with trends and fashion."

Consumers in China express a self-consciousness about the fact that mobile phones serve much more than just functional needs. Yi Wen, a 29-year-old Shanghainese woman who works in an ad agency, put it this way:

> My mobile phone is not only a tool for work and a necessity in my life. It is just like a jewel box, filled with all of my most precious things. It gives me entertainment when I am traveling, it has all of my networks, it lets me share my experiences wherever I go. It reflects my self-esteem.

Mu Mu, a 32-year-old human resources director, put it in more drastic terms:

> My mobile phone contains both my internal and external lives. It has my friends' contacts and my business contacts. It has info on clothing, food, accommodation, and traveling. A phone in my hand can resolve anything. Without it, I would become a deaf, blind, and lonely person. I can't afford to lose it. It has become the essential thing in my life.

The phone thus makes visible what is invisible. In the case of consumers in China, mobile devices have come to represent the ability to tap into their networks wherever they are. First-time visitors to China often remark to me that they find etiquette around mobile phone usage so different from in the West. It is common to hear people speaking loudly on their phones, even if they are in a meeting, sharing a meal with others, or in otherwise tight physical spaces where everyone else can listen in. Such behaviors underscore a person's successful cultivation of *guanxi* – especially if the conversation is business oriented. I have personally heard many phone calls by people who happened to be near me in which sensitive business information was being talked about loudly. In addition to talking loudly, business professionals typically place their phones in front of them whenever they sit down with others, whether for business or personal reasons. While this is nothing unusual in and of itself, non-Chinese observers have noticed that this action is often done in an almost exaggerated way, with the person placing the phone front and center, rather than looking at it discreetly. This serves two purposes – one is to be conspicuous about the brand, especially if it is a coveted high-end phone such as an iPhone. The second is to signify that they possess an active network, and that they expect calls or messages to come in at any time. A phone that is constantly ringing or buzzing with updates signifies that one has cultivated a healthy *guanxi* network. Status is tied to the notion of being a very busy person.

A contact is not just a name on a phone list, but also a potential ally in multiple situations that require a highly personalized relationship. Furthermore, these social networks incorporate various spheres of life in China – work, leisure, and family. Unlike findings from mobile research in the USA, where it was found that people tend to define fairly rigid groupings for people (e.g., someone is either a colleague or friend or family), among Chinese phone users, a single contact is often thought of in multiple contexts. For example, a superior at work can be someone you do favors for, or who does favors for you in particular situations. The flexibility in these ways of thinking about one's phone contact list reflects the desire to maximize *guanxi*.

Chinese phone manufacturers have been quick to recognize the value of mobile phones as conspicuous symbols of accomplishment. Less beholden to international design standards, domestic designs have featured big speakers, allowing users to broadcast their conversations loudly to everyone around them, as well as extremely loud notification rings, so that no opportunities are missed. Mobile phone marketers have also noted that, in the Chinese market, there is a greater tendency than in other markets for consumers to purchase high-end phones while only using just a small portion of what they are capable of. One's phone should reflect what one aspires to be, and not necessarily where one is today.

The ownership of counterfeit phones has also dipped in the last decade. From the early to the mid 2000s, domestic knock-offs of globally renowned brands were popular, especially with consumers in smaller cities or the countryside, where income levels were lower. Models such as the "Blockberry" and "HiPhone" competed with authentic brands for consumer dollars. However, recent years have seen the slowing of such counterfeit products. Slightly more than 24 million fake or *shanzhai* phones were ordered in China in 2010, about half the number at the peak in 2007 (Pierson 2011). As consumers in China become more familiar with the differences between counterfeit and genuine products, they believe that buying fake reflects badly on the person. Authentic status means investing in the authentic brand. Daniel Makoski, designer at Motorola who previously lived and worked in the Beijing office of Microsoft, recalled an incident with his driver.

> I asked my driver what he wanted us to bring back from the USA for him, and he immediately said an iPhone 4. I was surprised, because I knew his salary and knew that an iPhone was not something he could

easily afford. But he insisted, and told me to make sure I brought it back to him in all of its original packaging. He wanted to be able to prove to everyone that it was real, not a knock-off.

In addition to mobile phones, the proliferation of social media has created new ways for upwardly mobile Chinese to express their *guanxi*. Today, the size and reach of one's network can be literally shown to others through social networking sites such as RenRen and Kaixin, business review sites such as *Dianping*, and microblogging sites such as *Weibo Sina*. In the chapter on Spaces, we explored the way these sites create opportunities for shared consumption and perpetual connections. In addition, these sites create new imagined communities (Anderson 1983) transcending the direct, face-to-face relationships that make up pre-internet *guanxi* networks. People can expand their networks by becoming "star" microbloggers, focusing on points of views on topics such as beauty, health, or technology. Gu Hui, the unmarried professional we met in an earlier chapter who constantly moved back and forth between face-to-face and online conversations, was proud to become a "VIP reviewer" on *Dianping* – meaning that her posts about food went out to a wide audience. She was proud of her reputation on *Dianping*, and it gave her social capital among her colleagues at work, who began to see her as an expert in pop culture, and asked her opinion about food, fashion, and music.

THEORETICAL CONSIDERATIONS

A discussion about status in China inevitably brings up the question of whether a "real" middle class is forming, and how big this group is. The idea of a growing middle class, with the ability to purchase homes and cars, take vacations, and indulge in occasional luxury items, has come to dominate popular discourse on China's consumer market. Even a cursory examination of business titles related to China reveals that there is a lot of interest in defining and quantifying China's middle class. But this is a much more complex endeavor than it appears to be, as class is not a neutral term with a fixed definition in China. Under Mao Zedong's rule, class was defined for political purposes, separating those with the "right" background and mindset from those with corrupt, bourgeois thinking. In the last two decades, the idea of class has largely become depoliticized, as corporations and marketing professionals seek to define class through objective measures around salary, and subjective measures around lifestyle.

The concept of class, and especially a middle class, is ultimately limiting due to the fact that consumers in China do not themselves define social distinctions in terms of class. When confronted with the idea of middle classness, their drastically varying definitions underlie the reality that class is not a structuring concept for consumers themselves – at least not in any consistent, meaningful way. People do not talk about striving to be middle class, nor do they frame their aspirations and consumption choices in such terms. Rather, middle-class identity, at least in this period of time, is primarily a marketing concept, created and sustained by producers themselves who seek to understand and explain consumer activity with a kind of universal shorthand. While I do not deny the appeal of trying to relate what is happening in China to what has happened in the mature consumer markets of the West, we also need to think beyond familiar frameworks in order to account for the particular dynamics at play.

Mark Liechty's work on middle-class identity in Nepal as a *process* rather than a fixed concept provides an important framework for how to understand social distinctions in China. Liechty argues that class cannot be taken for granted as a natural, universal category. Rather, a deep understanding requires describing the experience of class in everyday life. As he puts it, it is the process, not the product, that constitutes class (2003: 15). We can extend his argument to apply to social distinctions more generally, given that middle classness has little salience in Chinese consumers' lives. Like Liechty's Nepalese subjects, the Chinese consumers explored in this book are creating social distinctions in their everyday activities, rather than adhering to a static notion of status.

What is clear is that consumers in China resist the notion of a fixed social hierarchy. This stems largely from the "clean slate" that resulted from Mao Zedong's drastic policies, effectively destroying the traditional elite. The younger generations thus find themselves searching for ways to express status without a socially entrenched elite to model themselves after. Building upon Liechty's call for us to focus on the everyday ways that status is experienced, I argue that what we see in China is an emerging form of status building based on what I call "conspicuous accomplishment." This idea has at its core the same principle of Veblen's original concept of conspicuous consumption in that people conspicuously surround themselves with specific symbols in order to demonstrate status. But the idea differs in that what consumers in China seek to demonstrate is not a sense of effortless wealth, but rather, the sense that they have earned their status through entrepreneurialism, hard work, or ingenuity. The display of *guanxi*, or one's social capital, for example, is one such way in which accomplishment is made conspicuous. It is the potential for change, and not the appearance of inherited privilege, which elicits the most admiration in China. The people who display such upward mobility are creating new markers of status. Yet these signs of status are in themselves also evolving as consumers in China continually redefine what "success" means.

By expanding on Veblen's original concept, we avoid applying views of class and status formation that are based on evidence derived from very different social and historical contexts. Signs of status in China today are being formed in a context in which there is no long-standing, entrenched elite class serving as a definitive guide to the tastes and lifestyles of the wealthy. What we see, instead, is the desire to be productive and to broadcast the ability to continually improve one's conditions. The desire to not be defined by static markers of class, but rather, be recognized for continuous striving and upward mobility, is at the heart of Chinese consumers' everyday experiences of status making.

4 | Lifestyles

When we met in 2012, Xie Yan Zuo was a 21-year-old copywriter for an ad agency in Mianyang, a third-tier city in Sichuan province. She lived with her parents, who moved to the city from the countryside when she was a little girl. Although she had just started working, she had big hopes for her career, and envisioned herself one day buying a new house for her parents. She also had very specific dreams for herself.

> I hope to have a Jeep Wrangler in the future. When I was small, I saw soldiers driving by, driving a Jeep. It made me feel so secure, I immediately wanted one. I still don't own a car but I have joined the cross-country vehicle club. Some own cars and others do not, but we all share a passion for cross-country cars. I read all the news I can about the Wrangler. I hope to have my own in the next five years.

When I pressed her to talk more about why she was so interested in owning a Jeep versus any other car, her reply surprised me in that she did not focus on the functional aspects of the car. Rather, she spoke about the role of the Jeep in helping her attain the lifestyle towards which she aspired.

> I hope to experience the grassland lifestyle of Inner Mongolia, a place where I can speak loudly without bothering anyone. I want to take nice pictures in Phuket Island and to see the deserts of Xinjiang. I like traveling because it enables me to see beautiful scenes and weird and

strange things on the road. I want to be surprised. For me, the Jeep Wrangler represents freedom and passion. That is what I am pursuing in my life. I will drive it to the mountains, to the grassland, and to the desert. My Jeep will drive me to freedom.

When I first lived in China in the early 1990s, the expectations of young adults for their futures focused primarily on financial stability. They hoped to have the opportunity to get good educations and then to be able to find lucrative salaried work once they finished school. By the early 2000s, teens and young adults had more ambitious desires for their futures. They spoke about fulfilling careers and owning their own homes and cars. In recent years, a new theme has emerged, especially among young adults of the *jiulinghou* generation (born in the 1990s). This theme revolves around creating a self-fulfilling, meaningful lifestyle. While consumption plays a central role, it is not about consumption for the sake of having more stuff in their lives. Rather, consumption facilities the realization of higher level, meaningful experiences. In her fantasies around owning and driving a Jeep, Xie Yan Zuo articulated a deeply felt connection between owning a particular product and her own growth and exploration. Driving a Jeep will, as she put it, help her to experience freedom and passion.

I asked her what her parents thought of her lifestyle, and she giggled and reminded me that they were from the countryside, and very conservative because of that.

My parents could not teach me how to enjoy life because they didn't grow up thinking it was possible or important. They cannot understand why I spend money on things they think can be purchased more cheaply or that we could do without. So I hide how much I spend from them, so they don't nag me. I like to eat out. They prefer to cook to save money. I like to buy the best brands. They settle for out-of-date technology. I want to feel happy. They are still focused on saving every penny, even though those hard times are over. That's their attitude and understanding towards life. They sacrificed their own life for the sake of others. My generation thinks about our own lives. It's not selfishness but a new attitude towards life. Compared with my parents, I live in the present and enjoy life. The generation of my parents lived a hard life. When they had enough time and money, the world didn't belong to them any longer. It's good to live in the present and enjoy our life. Like mountain climbing, we just enjoy the process of climbing. Whether we can get to the top and view the scenery is secondary.

This chapter explores how consumers in China – especially young adults – are crafting new lifestyles based on self-fulfillment, experimentation, and exploration. In framing themselves in terms of a particular lifestyle, consumers gather around objects or experiences which define their identity and become centerpieces of particular social routines (Slater 1997). The concept of lifestyle thus differs from other forms of social difference based on class, family, gender, and ethnicity (Shields 1992; Chaney 1996). It stresses cultural patterns made up of signs, representations, and media. Second, it is less permanent and stable, and more prone to change than traditional status affiliations because of its strong relationship with consumer choice (Miller et al. 1998).

Lifestyle choices can thus be thought of in relation to identity formation and experimentation. The view I take in this book borrows from postmodern social sciences, namely critical anthropology, feminist studies, and cultural studies, which posits that identity is flexible rather than fixed (Ong 1999). People move between different kinds of subjectivities, including their gender, class, generation, and lifestyle affiliations. In this view, a person does not simply "have" or "possess" a singular identity. Rather, identities are manipulated, and are better thought of in terms of politics as opposed to inheritance (Clifford 1992: 116). Decisions that people make about consumption – where they shop, what brands they wear, what car they drive – can change or reinforce perceptions of self. Identities and lifestyles, as seen through the lens of consumption, are dynamic and constantly changing (Arnould et al. 2004: 436). As Zukin argues, experimentations with lifestyle affiliations became one of the outcomes of the new consumer era. "Lifestyle emerged in the pages of consumer guides as a way to reconcile two types of shopping: shopping to associate ourselves with a set of collective qualities like social status, and shopping to advance a set of individual qualities, like beauty or pleasure, related to the self" (2004: 195).

I focus on the *jiulinghou* generation in this chapter because they are the first generation to have grown up fully within the reform period. They are the first generation to always have had internet access. They are a Singleton generation – only children under the One-Child Policy – growing up in conditions that their parents and grandparents had never experienced before. They have more spending power than any generation before them, and on top of that, are the sole focus of their grandparents and parents – at least until they marry, move out, and have children of their own. They are, by any objective standards, utterly unique in China's recent history. They are described in various ways by themselves and their elders – as bold, individualistic, self-centered, lonely, and materialistic. While there is disagreement as to whether their uniqueness is a privilege or handicap, what most Chinese agree upon is that they are creating a new philosophy towards life, and attempting to design new lifestyles based on this philosophy.

INDULGENCE

Mao Zedong would surely roll over in his grave if he knew how young adults are using the term petite bourgeoisie in China today. Yun Yue was a first-year student in university who lived with her parents and, by her account, desires more than anything else a lifestyle of leisure and indulgence.

My dream is to run an elegant and sweet café with my best friend, where we make our favorite cakes, bake sweet bread, and hold cups of hot chocolate in our hands. I wonder whether my parents would support my dream or not. Such a dream sounds unrealistic or crazy in the eyes of the adults. My friends are all outgoing and indulge in eating, drinking, and pleasure-seeking. They're interested in everything new. We are the *xiaozi* generation (*petite bourgeoisie*). My parents are the typical generation of the 1960s, who sometimes nag too much. We long for more than they ever dared to.

Everyone in China these days is pursuing a higher meaning in life, but most people do so just by being too busy. I will seek a higher meaning by leading a *xiaozi* lifestyle. I'll go traveling in my leisure time to make more friends. I'll have coffee and read novels.

I asked a friend of Yun Yue's, another self-described *xiaozi*, to tell me more about the *xiaozi* lifestyle.

A *xiaozi* lifestyle means spending most of one's salary. Living such a life in China is happy. You give yourself more relaxation. If you are not *xiaozi*, you can't get much relaxation. The lifestyle releases you from the burden of work. And it is composed of many elements. First, you need an open life attitude. You need to have a circle of friends who identify with your living philosophy.

The term *xiaozi* was first introduced under Mao Zedong's leadership, referring to shopkeepers and small business owners – not the big owners of the means of production, but people who needed to be re-educated, nonetheless. The term has resurged in the last few years among China's youth generation. Their use of it, however, is completely depoliticized. Instead of referring to a particular economic class, they use it to represent a way of living based on indulgence – eating good food, spending time with friends, buying things that one desires, and exhibiting a kind of creative coolness. Some have compared it to the Western term "yuppies" in the sense that it reflects a keen interest in material possessions. I would argue, however, that *xiaozi* reflects more of a philosophical outlook on life rather than a checklist of must haves. Being *xiaozi* is about being open to recognizing one's desires and willing to design a lifestyle that is self-fulfilling.

While not all young consumers associate themselves with the *xiaozi* lifestyle, the value placed on indulgence does resonate across China's young adults. Recognizing, naming, and acting on personal desire have only very recently become somewhat socially acceptable. In pre-Mao, traditional Chinese society, Confucian-influenced values around filial piety and self-sacrifice for the group pervaded social norms. Under Mao Zedong, the state sought to monitor and control personal lives to the extent that they expected the CCP's goals to pervade individual desires and inspire individual action. The topic, thus, of Chinese individuals being capable of expressing individual desires that may be in conflict with familial expectations or social norms has engendered a fair amount of scholarship. Some academics have argued that true individualism is not possible in China due to Confucian values as well as a recent history in which those who expressed their individuality were punished. Others reject the dichotomous framework of structure versus agency, arguing that people constantly move between the two, depending on the context, and that they can strategically frame individualistic choices in the language of group harmony to achieve their goals (Doctoroff 2012; Griffiths 2013).

Regardless of whether it comes from a "truly" individualistic space, young consumers are increasingly framing their lifestyles and aspirations in the language of desire. Lisa Rofel, in her work on urban residents and rural migrants in Hangzhou and Beijing, argues that the creation of such "desiring subjects" is at the core of China's economic development (2007). The state creates desiring subjects by encouraging consumption and, more specifically in the late 2000s, encouraging the use of credit cards. Consumers are thus encouraged through structural conditions to give in to their consumer fantasies in the present moment. In addition to the state, corporate marketing programs also teach consumers the language and imagery of indulgence.

Haagen-Dazs, the premium ice-cream maker, is an example of a brand that has capitalized on indulgence and succeeded despite concerns over their high prices and the fact that dairy products are relatively new to the Chinese market. The Haagen-Dazs store in Shanghai is not the typical casual ice-cream parlor found in the West. Rather, it was designed as a luxury space, situated near other luxury brands such as Louis Vuitton and Cartier on Nanjing Road. The ambiance suggests a European patisserie, and the prices are significantly higher than in the USA, with a banana split costing about $12. The all-dessert menu even has the word "Indulgence" on the cover. Young couples and families go to Haagen-Dazs, not to buy a pint to bring home and eat, but to linger in the environment and, given the fact that the store has all glass windows facing the main boulevard, to consume very conspicuously. Not surprisingly, Haagen-Dazs was one of the most mentioned brands when I asked young consumers in my study to name companies that represented the kind of indulgence they aspired towards.

Other forms of indulgence that have gained popularity include pampering the body. I heard numerous references to going to the spa, having a face or foot massage, or getting one's hair done as examples of how people, especially young women, indulge in their desires for physical pampering. Spending money in restaurants – especially luxurious places such as Haagen-Dazs – has become another important form of indulgence. Those who profess a *xiaozi* lifestyle talk about sitting in cafés, daydreaming. Young professionals mentioned hiring cleaning services so that they could spend less time doing housework, and more time enjoying life. As we'll explore further in a later chapter, the phenomenon of indulging children through buying them the very best foods, toys, and education characterizes the increasingly commodified nature of childhood.

The changing expectations around expressing and fulfilling desire causes tension between generations, however. In framing themselves as desiring individuals, young adults draw a contrast with their parents and grandparents.

> I'm often nagged at by my parents. When they were younger, life was so hard. They labored in the fields day after day and year after year. They paid for their children's food, clothing, and schooling on a small income. They lived frugally and gave their children the best in the hope that their children could make it and earn more money one day.

Yi Wen, aged 29, went on to describe the conflict she encountered when it came to indulging:

> In my view, high-quality products and services are worth the price. For example, while eating in a fancy restaurant, we can enjoy the nice environment, good taste, and superior service. However, my parents just can't understand why we spend so much money on that. As their daughter, I want my hard-working parents to enjoy the dinner, but their hearts ache for the money I spend. Most children like me won't let them know how much we have spent on the dinner. It's so pleasant to taste the sweet afternoon tea and bathe in the sunshine. However, my parents will pour cold water on me by saying that they'd rather have tea at home than waste money, which immediately lets me down.

Fulfilling desire is not just about acquiring goods, however. Young Chinese consumers also desire experiences that make them feel pampered and part of something special. During one set of ethnographies I conducted on shopping habits, I asked every participant to show me what was in their wallets and purses. This exercise is actually a lot of fun, as wallets and bags can carry some very revealing items about people. I was amazed to find that most people carried over a dozen loyalty cards and VIP cards, which their owners were very proud to have.

"Being a VIP member makes me feel special. I get a free gift and special treatment," said Feng Sha Chen, a wealthy 41-year-old woman who really did not need any freebies, but appreciated being treated differently. Marketers new to China are always astounded at how ubiquitous loyalty programs are, and how quickly they have proliferated in a still growing market. VIP cards, free gifts with a purchase, and loyalty perks are not just nice to haves, but have become central to the Chinese consumer experience. This idea of being "special" is the antithesis of the consumer experience during the Maoist period, when expressions of social distinctions were considered counter-revolutionary.

This idea of living in the present contrasts with perceptions young people have of their parents' lifestyles. The older generation is portrayed as always worrying about the future, deferring gratification, and saving for emergencies as opposed to spending now. Young adults often complain to me that their parents are too self-sacrificing. In contrast, they display a desire to be in the moment. But their definition of being in the moment is often tied to immediate consumer gratification. Being in the present is defined as spending in the moment. Giving in to one's immediate, emotional desires is an important, central part of their identity as modern, post-socialist subjects. Younger consumers believe that by giving in to desire, they can tap into their authentic selves.

> The lifestyle I am after is also a cultured one. I want to seek out elegant hobbies, like theater and ballet, painting, and collecting antiques. I want to balance that with outdoors sports like skiing and golf. I want to understand the abundant history and cultural knowledge of other countries, and master several languages by studying overseas. I want to enrich both my body and my mind. I am far away from this lifestyle now, but I hope to achieve it in the next ten years.

Yi Wen, the 29-year-old ad agency strategist we met earlier, wanted more than just to be able to afford luxury products. She wanted to be a learned person. As a reaction to Veblen's concept of conspicuous consumption, Pierre Bourdieu argued that money spent on one's lifestyle was not the only criterion for demonstrating superior status. In addition, he pointed to good taste in food, art, music, literature, and home décor as vehicles for demonstrating one's cultural capital (1984). Good taste, as Bourdieu observed, did not necessarily correlate with the most conspicuous forms of consumption. Someone who showed off their wealth excessively without displaying the right markers of refined taste would not be considered part of the superior class.

Among consumers in China, the idea of *pinwei*, or "good taste," connotes a person of high quality (*suzhi*). As anthropologist Ann Anagnost argues, this concept "articulates the boundaries of China's newly differentiating social strata" (2004: 190). *Pinwei* has thus become the outward marker of the internal quality of *suzhi*, manifesting itself, as Bourdieu posited, in people's consumption habits.

Markers of good taste, however, have not remained static over the last thirty years in China. The social upheaval brought on by the CCP and its goal of a classless society destroyed the traditionally entrenched upper class. Post-1978, the political elite, who also represented a substantial percentage of the economic elite, did not become models of good taste for the upwardly mobile or the masses.

NEO-TRIBES

When we first met, Yang Xiao Kang was a 19-year-old university student, living with her parents in a suburb of Shanghai. She was participating in a study I was conducting on teens and fashion. She considered herself "*linglei*," or alternative, which she expressed through a pierced nose and her frizzy, dyed blonde hair. She proudly showed me every outfit in her closet, which included ripped shirts, a hot pink miniskirt, tight black faux leather pants, and platform boots. Despite the "dark" look she strove for as part of her *linglei* identity, she had Hello Kitty barrettes on her dresser table, her walls were decorated with clean-cut Korean pop stars, and she spoke sweetly to her mother and grandmother when they brought fruit in for us to eat. Even with her platform boots on, she stood at barely five feet tall, but exuded a confidence and energy that more than made up for her height.

When I asked her what being *linglei* meant, her answer focused on her community. "My friends are all this way so I guess that is what binds us together. We have a passion for music, poetry, and fashion, and we want to live our life in a lifestyle that is free. We are all very smart but we don't want to focus on school as our only way to success." She then went on to show me, on her PC, how she kept in touch with her community:

> Many of the people who influence me the most are people I know online. I have never met them, but we share a like-minded approach to life. We don't want to spend our money on clothes from big brands. We prefer to seek out unusual items or used clothes, and create our own style. Then we share them with each other through our microblogs. I get ideas from them on how to personalize my clothes, like adding jeweled studs to my jeans.

Yang Xiao Kang's description of *linglei* surprised me in that while it had some aspects of rebellion, it was not, like punk culture in the West, fundamentally about defying the powers that be. Rather, the foundation of her *linglei* identity was in sharing a common consumption philosophy with others, based on a desire to experiment with alternative, de-branded styles. The last decade in China has seen the emergence of new social groups based on experimentations with fashion, brands, music, and other forms of consumer culture.

French sociologist Michel Maffesoli wrote that "identity is never, from the sociological point of view, anything but a simply floating and relative condition" (1996: 65). Instead of the fixed "older" forms of identity that sociologists had been concerned with (e.g., class, subcultures), he argued that contemporary consumers live "in the time of the tribes." These "neo-tribes," as he called them, are organized around brand affiliations and role-playing fantasies based on consumer choices. Consumer culture has thus created new forms of "sociality," which Maffesoli described as a highly unstable space where multiple tribal circles intersect and make meaning based on whatever is happening in the moment (1996: 97). Because of their dependence on consumer behavior, neo-tribes are fragile. They disperse as easily as they come together.

The concept of neo-tribes is useful in an exploration of the current climate of experimentation among China's youth and young adults, as they seek out new affinity groups based on their consumption practices. Pop culture fan clubs have exploded in popularity over the last two decades. QQ groups or other kinds of online forums command dedicated followings from Taiwanese boy bands to Japanese manga to Korean soap operas to Western teen sensations such as Taylor Swift. Participants on reality dating shows such as "If you are the one" become instant celebrities with their own following. Even China's first lady, Peng Liyuan, is the object of intense fan worship. In early 2013, several fan clubs emerged around her, including the Liyuan Fan Club, *Xuexileyuan* (Learn from Happy Yuan) and *Xuexiaiyuan* (Learn from Xi Love Yuan).

Other neo-tribes revolve around people's interest in specific products. Zhu Long, whom we met in the chapter on Spaces, enjoyed going to the Apple store to commune with other Apple fans, and to feel like he is in the presence of Steve Jobs. Xie Yan Zuo, the self-described obsessed fan of the Jeep automobile brand, spent her leisure time reading up on Jeep news and communing with other Jeep fans.

I am part of the cross-country vehicle club since I am a big Jeep fan. In the club, everyone is a fan of cross-country vehicles. Some people own these cars and others, like myself, just dream of them. We share our thoughts, get ideas, and make friends. When we're not meeting, we also chat together on QQ. Those who have off-road vehicles arrange for road trips that we can take together.

Other neo-tribes arise out of common interests around luxury goods. Affinity China, for example, is a private network which provides access to unique luxury, lifestyle, and travel opportunities for its members. They offer very exclusive opportunities for their members, which include private showings at fashion shows, trips to luxury resorts around the world via private jets, invitation-only dinners with five-star chefs, and access to art gallery openings. In one instance, Affinity China hosted a gala event for Chinese socialites, celebrities, and high level executives to participate in wine tasting and previewing select luxury brands, including a Lamborghini.

One of the fastest growing types of affinities revolves around outdoor activities, as sports and fitness become more increasingly commoditized. Skiing has become an aspirational sport in China. There are a handful of ski resorts, but skiing has yet to become popular with the masses due to the prices, difficulty in picking it up as a beginner, and reluctance to take vacations in such cold regions. Nonetheless, skiing has come to represent adventure, travel, and prosperity, as it is not a sport for everyone. Despite the very small number of skiers in China, ski wear appears in storefronts during the winter months, enticing consumers with the lifestyle associated with the sport. Golf had a similar beginning in China, although it has picked up in terms of popularity. Numerous golf courses have been built in Hainan province, attracting both domestic and international players. While it is prohibitively expensive for the majority, it is a top recreational sport for the wealthy. On the more adventurous side, I have also heard people mention bungee jumping and rock climbing as activities they want to try.

In addition to adventure sports, people in China are also beginning to experiment with other forms of physical expression and exercise, including yoga and salsa dancing. Since the late 2000s, salsa has become increasingly popular in China's big urban areas, as people learn and experience the dance form in the various Latin dance studios that have opened up. One woman I spoke with mentioned how free salsa made her feel – sexual and seductive, unlike anything she had ever experienced before. Indeed, the desire to learn salsa extends beyond the desire for exercise and sociality. In a country where social dance was condemned as a bourgeois practice under Mao Zedong and overt forms of feminine sexuality were condemned, it allows people to experiment with physical expressions of passion and eroticism. Similarly, in less than a decade, yoga studios have sprouted up all over China. They rival gyms and other traditional exercise studios for the dollars and time of professional women, who are looking for both a way to stay slim but also the sense of belonging and community that yoga studios tend to foster.

Young Chinese are also experimenting with "do it yourself" hobbies. This includes making their own jewelry, pottery, clothing, and accessories. Among young women, this DIY trend reflects a couple of motivations. The first is the desire to save money. The second is the desire to create something unique for one's self – not available in any store. This may take the form of a self-design print on a shirt or a recycled handbag decorated with rhinestones. While still niche, DIY culture reflects a growing desire for options beyond mass-produced fashions and other forms of adornment. DIY culture is also spreading quickly through social media, as netizens share their designs and creations with their networks, and in turn, spur others to try their hand at handicrafts and the like. DIY culture challenges the notion of consumers as passively consuming, and opens up the possibility of framing individuals as hybrid consumer-makers. Teenager Mi Li Ting described her delight over sharing her cooking experiments.

> Several days ago I read a blog on how to make glutinous rice rolls with sweet bean flour. I had time today, so I tried to make it. Although my rolls didn't look very nice, they were tasty. The important thing is that I did it on my own without the help of my friends or parents. Before eating them, I took some pictures and uploaded them on my microblog. My friend saw it, and she said I should share it with *Weixin* (a mobile phone app). I downloaded it, and it is so much easier to share my photos with friends now.

Younger Chinese are clearly at the forefront of creating and participating in neo-tribes, but those in older generations are also experimenting with new activities and forms of sociality that support their interests. Mi Li Ting described how she got turned on to kite flying by an elderly man:

> We took a walk along the bank of the Huangpu River. Many kites were lit up with LEDs and flew across the sky. An old man was about to fly a kite so I went over to him. When we were about to leave, the old man gave us information about a QQ group, an online discussion group made up of amateurs who like flying kites. I joined this group and over time they became my friends.

While fan clubs in and of themselves are not unique to consumer cultures around the world, what is significant is the intensity of Chinese fans' interest and time spent online, communing with other fans. Fan sites become communities that span geography, linking participants that would otherwise have no other points of contact. While, as Maffesoli argues, these neo-tribes may disperse as quickly as they form, in my research I have found that connections made through fanship are often carried over into other arenas. Xie Yan Zuo, for example, transitioned some of her online friendships in the Jeep club into face-to-face relationships, which then eventually became friendships that went beyond their common passion.

QQ is especially appropriate for these online, potentially fleeting associations based on common interests. The service allows people to sign up without revealing their real identity – most create a nickname that often reflects a particular neo-tribe affiliation. QQ groups thus are constructed as fluid spaces where people can meet and communicate. QQ users typically start chatting with others online, in the multitude of forums based on common interests. They may even choose to play some games together, or share links to music or websites featuring their topic of interest. When they decide they want to take their relationships to the next stage, they transition these contacts into other social networking sites, which are made up of more intimate social circles. As Herold and Marolt write, "The internet is never just a technological product – it always has a socio-cultural dimension" (2011: 37).

As consumers in China discover new brands, products, and services, they are also experimenting with new lifestyle affinities. These are, as Maffesoli argues, less stable than traditional sociological groupings, based on ethnicity, race, class, or other subcultures (1996). Nonetheless, despite their potential fleeting and flexible nature, these new affiliations are deeply significant. As Yang Xiao Kang demonstrates, *linglei* is not so much of a description as an ongoing set of social practices, connecting her to people, content, and imagined lifestyles.

COSMOPOLITANISM

During the years under Mao Zedong's rule, every citizen was assigned a geographical location to which they belonged. They were either urban or rural, and within this divide, they belonged to a *danwei* or an agricultural commune. Changing one's geographical assignment, or *hukou*, was virtually impossible, and this assignment had an immense impact on a person's lifestyle and livelihood. Rural residents were not allowed to move to the city to seek work. State officials also used geographical assignments as punishment. Those who were called out as counter-revolutionary were typically sent to remote rural regions for "re-education." Being sent to the countryside thus became synonymous with being punished.

Travel outside China was virtually impossible. Only those at the highest level of the government and a select number of experts were allowed out of the country. For the most part, travel was restricted to countries with socialist regimes, such as the (then) Soviet Union and some African nations. The prohibitive costs of travel and restrictive state policies kept the vast majority of Chinese nationals at home until the early 2000s. But people's imaginations were stoked by the ever-increasing number of expatriates, tourists, and foreign-exchange students that started to enter China in the early 1980s. I remember when I lived in Beijing as a foreign-exchange student in 1990, my local friends were hungry for any kind of cultural knowledge. They wanted to exchange language lessons but, more importantly, they wanted us to bring to life for them what it was like to live in the US. Back then, I felt the incredible disparity between our experiences. We, as fairly privileged American exchange students, never doubted that we had the right and the capacity to travel abroad. My Chinese friends, on the other hand, had only very distant hopes that they could ever travel beyond China's borders. The 1989 Tiananmen crackdown made it even more difficult for students to obtain permission to travel abroad.

Conditions have changed dramatically. Since the early 2000s an increasing number of Chinese have traveled outside China. China is now the world's fourth-largest outbound travel market, and in 2012, the United Nations World Tourism Organization predicted that the number of overseas trips made by Chinese people will surge to 100 million by the end of the decade, up from only five million just fifteen years ago. In 2013, Chinese tourists overtook the Germans to become the world's biggest-spending travelers in the world, according to the World Tourism Organization (Kane and Bryan 2013). Popular destinations for the majority of travelers include Hong Kong, Macau, South Korea, and Thailand. Although inbound tourists from China are still restricted, Taiwan has also become a popular destination. For those at the higher end of the economic spectrum who can afford to travel further out, Dubai, Paris, and Sydney are typically on the dream list. Even the Maldives has become a popular beach destination, especially for honeymooners. This desire is inspired by an ever-broadening number of travel magazines, travel TV shows, and access to foreign media showcasing foreign lifestyles.

This very recent ability to travel has come to mean many things to consumers in China. The freedom to cross borders, whether geographical, cultural, or imaginary, symbolizes the spatial freedom that was denied to them for several decades. Travel is, as was explored in the chapter on Status, also a marker of social mobility. People who travel increase their cultural capital, and their potential for business and social success. Travel has become one marker of a consumer-oriented lifestyle.

As the tourism industry has developed in China, the desire for destinations has become more diverse. When I first started doing research in China, most people talked about the USA, Australia, and Europe as their ideal travel destinations. Once travel became accessible to more people, the nearer countries of East Asia came onto people's radar, fueled by the interest in pop culture, fashion, and cuisines from China's neighbors. More recently, I have heard people mention a greater range of faraway destinations, including Greece, India, and Africa. China has become South Africa's fourth-largest tourist source market. The interest in Africa stems in part from Chinese direct investments, as China has replaced the USA as Africa's largest trade and investment partner (*Global Times* 2013).

At the other end of the spectrum is the boom in luxury tourism, centered primarily on travel for the sake of purchasing expensive items. As Renee Hartmann, co-founder of China Luxury Advisors observes, China's upper class fly to places like Paris, not to see the Mona Lisa, or to taste the macaroons, but to engage in shopping. The average Chinese traveler to Europe spends US$15,000 on each trip. Tour group itineraries include day-long trips to luxury retail outlets, where travelers can snatch up luxury items at a lower cost than in China, which has high import taxes on such goods. Other luxury shopping destinations include Las Vegas and, most recently, Dubai. Dubai's Mall of the Emirates has become a desired destination for its portfolio of high-fashion brand stores, including Armani, Balenciaga, Bottega Veneta, Coach, Dolce & Gabanna, and Gucci. As Gottdiener puts it, "many travel vacations are, in reality, shopping trips" (2000b: 269).

The increased mobility of Chinese tourists has not only affected the consumption behaviors of the tourists themselves, it is beginning to affect the international tourist industry. As anthropologist James Clifford argues, not only do tourists travel, but their cultures travel as well (1992). Destinations have begun to change in order to accommodate Chinese lifestyles. For example, hotels in top-tier destinations such as Paris and Dubai are starting to employ Chinese-speaking staff. They are also offering Chinese breakfasts of congee or noodles, hot water thermoses and slippers in the rooms, and Chinese language TV. Observing that Chinese tourists are more interested in spending their money on shopping than on amenities, lower-price hotels near shopping districts are selling themselves heavily to Chinese tour groups.

With such changes in the make-up of global tourism, there have also been cultural conflicts as Chinese travelers challenge international travel norms. French fashion designer Thierry Gillier caused an outrage in China when he was quoted as saying that he did not want Chinese tourists in his luxury hotel. He apologized and clarified that what he meant was that he did not want his hotel to cater to mass tourism, but the remark underscored the newness of Chinese travel around the world, and the cultural disconnects that have emerged. In 2013, the Maldives came under social media criticism in China after it was alleged that Chinese tourists were discriminated against at one upscale resort. The core of the outrage centered on the allegation that hotel management had hot-water kettles removed from the rooms of Chinese guests in order to discourage in-room cooking of instant noodles and lobsters purchased at the seafood markets.

Perhaps nowhere have the tensions been higher than in Hong Kong, which, despite being technically part of the People's Republic, is still economically and politically a separate entity. The increase in Mainland Chinese tourism into Hong Kong has contributed to a growing culture clash between Mainland Chinese and residents of the former British colony. Local Hong Kong consumers complain that their shopping spaces are being overrun and abused. They accuse Mainland Chinese tourists of improper behavior, including talking too loudly in public spaces, not flushing toilets, and spitting on the streets. In January 2012, video captured a dispute between a Hong Kong subway rider and a Mainland Chinese family, when the former pointed out to the latter that there was no eating allowed on the train. The dispute caused a social media frenzy because of the heated words and, perhaps more importantly, the fact that the scene demonstrates the uncomfortable relationship between Hong Kong and the rest of China. Up until recently, the residents of Hong Kong were considered economically and culturally superior. The influx of rich Mainland Chinese into the city has upset this view, contributing to tensions as the relationship between Chinese across borders gets played out in this form of tourism.

Other Chinese are seeking not only to travel but also to obtain foreign residency. The primary destinations have included North America, where elite Chinese hope to be able to send their children to school as well as invest in real estate. More recently, Hong Kong,

Singapore, and cash-strapped European countries such as Cyprus have also become sought-out destinations for foreign residency. The motivations behind the desire to have one foot in China, and another abroad, so to speak, are varied. Those with children see themselves as investing in the educational opportunities of the latter. Those with large financial holdings are attracted to the security of stable economies and seek to invest their wealth outside China (Ong 1997, 1999).

In addition to travel, consumers seek other forms of engagement with the world outside China's borders. Since 1979, the presence of foreign companies, products, media, and expatriate workers has drawn China into globally interdependent economic and cultural webs. While the state continues to limit foreign influence through censorship of sensitive political topics (which we will explore more in the chapter "Awareness"), the population's interaction with ideas and inventions from outside China has grown exponentially. What consumers in China are seeking, beyond physical travel itself, is to live a cosmopolitan lifestyle. Here, I borrow Stuart Hall's definition of cosmopolitanism, as ". . . the ability to stand outside having one's life written and scripted by any one community, whether that is a faith or tradition or religion or culture – whatever it might be – and to draw selectively on a variety of discursive meanings" (2002).

Another way in which consumers in China express their cosmopolitanism is through foreign-language acquisition. In the last two decades, foreign-language learning has boomed in China. Foreign-language learning is already an integral part of the Chinese public educational system, with students learning English as early as the first grade. Private-language learning schools have capitalized on the high interest in language fluency, offering a variety of online and in-class options for children and adults. As in other parts of Asia, there are strong preferences for teachers who are native speakers, even if their teaching skills are subpar to their Chinese colleagues who are better trained as foreign-language instructors. What the students desire is not just the language learning itself, but also the additional cultural learning they feel they are getting by communicating with a foreign teacher. They seek not just language proficiency, but cultural proficiency. Especially ambitious students form English language clubs or go to the park for English language practice time.

What motivates language learners is the association between English and professional success. Most students I spoke with believe that working for a multi-national corporation is more prestigious than working for the state or for a domestic company. This stems from the belief that international companies pay better, are better run, and most importantly, provide exposure to innovative business and technology practices. There is also the belief that Western companies allow their employees more creative freedom and opportunities to stand out.

Cosmopolitan practices can also take more everyday forms that do not require as heavy financial investments as traveling or migrating abroad. As we explored in the chapter on Spaces, going to foreign restaurants is thought of as a way to engage with the world, learn about different cultures, and practice interacting with different forms of modernity. Foreign TV shows such as *Gossip Girl* have become popular among China's young women, in particular, and are often the source of fashion trends. *Youku* and *Tudou*, China's equivalents to YouTube, offer a growing library of licensed Hollywood TV content. Shows such as *Desperate Housewives*, *Glee*, *Survivor*, *Gossip Girl*, and *America's Got Talent* are readily available to anyone with an online connection. Hollywood movies are often available in China through pirated DVDs and peer-to-peer online networks.

Although Chinese engagement with foreign culture is often framed in terms of Western culture, and most often, US culture, in the last decade there has been growing interest in the lifestyles of certain Asian countries – in particular, Japan, South Korea, and Taiwan. For the Chinese, these places represent "modern Asia," and alternative forms of consumer culture that they can experience through music, TV shows, fashion magazines, and the blogosphere. Demonstrating one's connection to these foreign cultures, whether through language, fashion, education or travel, has become an important marker of social distinction.

In fact, record numbers of Chinese tourists are visiting East Asian destinations such as Seoul and Tokyo. The Global East represents forms of modernity that consumers in China see as "closer" to what they are striving for. As Yi Wen, the ad agency strategist, puts it:

> Asian countries are closer to us, so information can spread faster and more conveniently. We can go traveling and shopping in those cities any time, their influence on us is more direct. Western countries are far away from us, so we cannot go traveling and shopping at any time; and the spread of fashion trends and information is also slower. When it comes to new ideas, life habits, food, clothing, and skin care products, we get them faster from Asia than the West. They are also closer to us in terms of culture, so we can more easily accept and integrate them.

In particular, South Korean culture has had a growing presence in China since the late 1990s. Chinese consumer interest in Korean pop, or k-pop, soap operas, movies, fashion, and celebrities has been dubbed the "Korean Wave." South Korea's TV novellas have swept China's imagination. Popular television dramas are broadcast both over the air and on internet TV in China. Korean superstars, including Kwon Sang-woo, Jang Seo-hee, and Jang Woo-hyuk, appear in Chinese dramas. K-pop artists such as Big Bang enjoy number one status on Chinese music charts. Korean movies, such as *Late Autumn*, starring Hyun Bin, become instant hits at the box office. Korean stars such as Rain have also become the obsession of teenage girls in China, and in several household ethnographies I found posters of him lovingly taped to bedroom walls. In addition to pop culture, South Korean technology brands are cited as proof by consumers in China that innovation can happen outside the West. Samsung and LG are currently among the most popular brands for mobile phones, televisions, and home appliances.

Consumer interest in Korean pop culture stems from a mix of admiration for Korea as well as a perception that Korean and Chinese culture share certain characteristics. As one woman in her fifties put it:

> I watch South Korean TV series with my daughter. I love the clothes. I love the phones they use in the shows – so modern and distinctive. I also appreciate how South Koreans are not arrogant, they know how to be grateful to others. Tradition runs deep in their culture. I think we share many aspects in common with them.

Perceptions of Japan, however, are more complex. On the one hand, since economic reforms, an ever-increasing array of Japanese products has become available in China. Japanese technology, in particular, is often thought of as superior to any domestic or Western brands. Japanese cosmetics brands, such as Shiseido, enjoy high prestige among female consumers. Japanese food is among the most popular among foreign cuisines in China's largest cities. At the same time, there is still a pervasive sense of distrust of the Japanese. Older Chinese have much stronger feelings, typically citing the Nanjing Massacre and what they feel is a history of hostility between the two nations. Younger Chinese tend to say that such historical events do not affect them, yet they do cite issues such as the dispute between China and Japan over the sovereignty of a set of islands, known as *Diaoyu* in China, as proof of Japan's aggression. In 2012, the tension between Beijing and Tokyo around the status of those islands erupted into consumer boycotts of Japanese products. At the height of tensions, Japanese cars were vandalized, and retailers took down Japanese products in their stores. Japanese manufacturers closed their factories for several weeks in order to protect their property and employees. Yet as quickly as these protests rose up, they also died down. In some research I conducted in late 2012 on conspicuous consumption, consumers in China were back to buying luxury Japanese products as if there had been no international tensions. As one young man in this study put it:

> Japan tries to bully China but we don't back down. But for ordinary people like me, this is of no concern to us. We respect Japanese technology and buy it when we can afford it because it is the highest quality. People who own Japanese technology are high-quality people themselves.

In recent years, I have also observed a growing interest in Greater China – namely Taiwan and Hong Kong. This interest in what is called *gangtai wenhua* (Gold 1993) reflects the growing desire among consumers to experience different Chinese lifestyles. Hong Kong and Taiwanese pop songs have, at least until the Korean wave, typically dominated the music charts in China. Hong Kong, with its history as a port city and colony of Great Britain, remains a gateway to technology and fashion trends, especially in southern China. Travel to Hong Kong is typically associated with shopping for luxury brands. Taiwanese food trends are especially popular in Shanghai, as young consumers sip bubble tea or try out Taiwanese tea house delicacies. Taiwanese make-up bloggers are among the most influential fashion icons for Chinese women. While still highly regulated, mainland travel to Taiwan has gradually opened up since 2011, allowing for some cultural exchanges.

Chinese consumer experiences are becoming increasingly influenced by not just one, but multiple centers of influence. The West, as a symbol of modernity, remains a powerful influence in terms of people's strategies for success, whether it is through language learning, conspicuous consumption of luxury brands, or obtaining foreign residency. The

Global East, however, has also exerted enormous influence on consumer desires and the framing of social status. Being a fan of the hippest pop stars, getting the best make-up advice, going to the coolest new restaurants in the city – all of these daily consumption activities are becoming increasingly influenced by the cultures of South Korea, Japan, and Greater China. These influences, in turn, are reworking Chinese identities and subjectivities, creating cosmopolitan, transnational Chinese consumer practices (Ong and Nonini 1997).

THEORETICAL CONSIDERATIONS

In this chapter, we have seen that young adults in China are aspiring towards and designing new lifestyles, crafting them out of their consumer choices. Such lifestyles differ dramatically from those that their parents and grandparents experienced throughout the decades under Mao Zedong's leadership. Leisure time has become privatized and de-politicized. Self-indulgence and self-fulfillment have grown in importance, as younger consumers seek both to distinguish themselves from the older generation, as well as to express themselves through consumption. The ability to cross cultural and geographical borders has become a significant marker of these new lifestyles, as tourists consume luxury goods, on one end of the spectrum, and idealized forms of rural tradition, on the other end of the spectrum.

From a theoretical perspective, the postmodern work that began in the 1980s gives us a foundation for understanding how consumers shape their own experiences. In *The Practice of Everyday Life* (1984), de Certeau argued that people are hardly passive recipients of meanings that producers create, but rather, they create their own meanings around commodities through everyday decisions and actions. He points out that in a closer look at the tactics people employ in their everyday lives, we can begin to uncover the way in which ordinary people potentially subvert the meanings that corporations seek to define for them. He called these the "tactics of consumption," giving rise to a more agent-oriented view of how consumers act. Everyday life, according to de Certeau, is a process of using but also subverting the rules that exist in culture.

De Certeau's influence on postmodern social theory was immense. Scholars shifted from a framework of alienation to one in which consumption was viewed as a democratic exercise, in which individuals could invent and reinvent themselves through their consumer choices. Instead of mass conformity, the postmodern scholars emphasized the use of commodities to construct individual, self-realized, resistant, and creative selves. The new agency-focused literature highlighted the ways in which people played with gender, ethnicity, and subordinated identities in ways that challenged and undermined structures of social domination (Featherstone 2007). Consumption was no longer positioned as something negative, a submission to the will of the corporations, but rather, as a space for pleasure, escape, enjoyment, and possibly even liberation. Consumers were thus depicted in terms of their resistant, liberatory, and creative tendencies (Schor and Holt 2000).

Michel Maffesoli's concept of neo-tribes adds another essential dimension to our analysis (1996). The notion of neo-tribes captures the shift from established ties based on lineage and geographical proximity, to ties based on everyday living. As Maffesoli argues, they are not fixed in the sense of traditional tribes, but can be formed spontaneously and can exist in stable or fleeting configurations. Individuals can affiliate with multiple neo-tribes, which provide sources of identity, however permanent or temporary. When viewed in light of postmodern theory, neo-tribes can be framed as liberatory in the sense that they provide alternative forms of identity that allow people to experiment outside the affiliations they are born into.

As we have seen in this chapter, membership in neo-tribes ranging from Jeep lovers to salsa dancers to *linglei* rebels constitutes a significant part of consumer experiences in China today. These neo-tribes span virtu-real contexts, as members commune and share ideas on QQ or affirm their "good taste" on sites such as Affinity China. Yet consumer-based neo-tribes in China can be thought of as more than just lifestyle affiliations. They are also forms of social capital (Bourdieu 1984). Membership in the Jeep club is about more than just sharing a love of certain automobiles. It is also about affiliating one's self with a network of fellow Jeep owners (and aspiring owners). In this sense, neo-tribes in consumer China often take on a branded nature. They revolve around specific corporate-based identities, whether they represent luxury or alternative lifestyles. Membership in such affinity groups signifies one's engagement with both the fellow members as well as the meaning of the brand. To be part of the Jeep club is to announce one's uninhibited, "free" lifestyle, and one's social capital through affiliation with like-minded people. But Maffesoli's original concept of neo-tribes recognized their fleeting nature, and in this sense, what we see in China is not the taking on of permanent new identities, but often temporary experimentations with branded affiliations.

Travel has become another form of cultural capital in China. The ability to cross cultural borders, whether they are international or between urban and rural within China, is viewed as a means to demonstrate one's physical and social mobility, and thus one's ability to consume the "other." But this desire for cosmopolitan forms of cultural capital entails more than the ability to demonstrate one is "cultured" because of access to Parisian boutiques and Japanese cuisine. The ability to travel also creates opportunities for access to foreign citizenship. And in this sense, a desire for cosmopolitan lifestyles can also stem from a desire to elude the control of the Chinese state. Aihwa Ong's concept of flexible citizenship as a form of transnationalism is informative in understanding the experience of Chinese consumers who seek residency in other countries (1999). In her work, Ong argues that acquiring passports in desirable, stable locations such as the United States, Canada, and Australia is in itself a form of capital that can be used for business and educational purposes. Foreign passport holders may not necessarily ever want to settle in their new countries of residence, but they use their privileges as citizens elsewhere to create new opportunities for themselves and their children. Nonetheless, the reality for the majority of citizens in China is a still restrictive state which does not allow people to travel freely across all borders, most notably into areas of contention such as Taiwan and Hong Kong.

Emerging Chinese lifestyles are thus best viewed as fragmented, plural, and inextricably linked to the market. Korean pop stars as well as well-heeled Parisians serve as models, but each only partially so. Consumers in China seem to be stitching together their own versions of desirable experiences, navigating between multiple forms of cosmopolitanism, generational gaps, and branded experiences. Consumers are re-appropriating concepts such as "petite bourgeoisie" to fit their own, emerging values around desire-fulfillment. Young adults are seeking to frame their experiences on their own terms, rejecting the self-sacrifice that they attribute to the older generations. Likewise, consumers in China are showing agency in their choices to explore new practices, such as more sexually expressive hobbies like salsa, as well as new online affiliations based on connections that span traditional boundaries. The presence of ski wear in the windows of luxury brand stores creates an association between a particular activity and a particular way of life. The desire for travel is heavily influenced by the strategic marketing of destinations in terms of luxury shopping, romantic getaways, "exotic" cultures, or rural authenticity. In seeking out new ways to live, people in China are experimenting with and creating multi-variate tactics of consumption.

5   Commodification ————————————

Chris Liu is a market research professional who lives in Shanghai and travels around the country, conducting studies on Chinese consumer habits for a variety of companies. When we first met in the early 2000s, he was just a few years out of school, and an eager young professional who put long hours into his work. We collaborated on various projects together in China, from mobile phone usage in first-tier cities, to the base of the pyramid lifestyles, to eating habits among children. As the decade progressed, Chris's own life also reflected different stages of consumer behavior. Once he turned thirty, he began to think seriously about marriage. But before he could even consider looking around for a wife, he had to buy a house and a car – the prerequisites for a man to marry in today's China. I asked him if he ever drove the car, and he said with all the traffic in Shanghai, it was easier to take the subway, but despite its impracticality, a car was still a necessity for marriage. Once those "must haves" were secured, he reconnected with an elementary school friend, and within a year they were married. They held their banquet at a mid-range hotel in Shanghai, which cost the equivalent of US$10,000.

When we met in early 2013, he and his wife were the proud parents of a little boy. Chris had also recently become a senior manager at his company. Despite all of his outward successes, Chris did reveal that keeping up with society's expectations around success did not get any easier. Now that they were parents, he and his wife felt immense pressure to buy their child the very best of everything. "Don't let your kids lose at the beginning" is a saying that pervades advertising around many child and infant-related products and services. What the saying means is that parents should not put their child at a disadvantage by not giving him or her what she needs to succeed in life. As Chris puts it, that may include anything from baby products, through after-school tutorials when they are older, to specialty foods marketed as nutritious for developing brains.

Chris's lifestyle reflects the enormous changes that market reform has brought about in terms of people's homes, relationships with potential spouses, and child rearing. While these areas of life are vastly different, what they share is that they have become increasingly commodified within the last two decades. The idea of commodification has its origins in Marxist political theory, and is used to describe the process by which something which once did not have an economic value becomes assigned such a value. As Marx intended, it also denotes a fundamental change in relationships, formerly untainted by commerce, into relationships with commercial characteristics. Marx focused on the commodification of the labor process, in which the actual activity of labor by individual workers became transformed into abstract labor, which could be measured in terms of hours and money.

However, discussions of commodification have extended to the cultural arena, especially in the context of advertising. Advertising often places commodities at the center of social relationships – the diamond engagement ring that signifies a couple's commitment or the fast-food meal that promotes quality time between parents and children. Images of social relationships playing out in positive ways mask the underlying market exchanges. Advertising thus disguises the production process, creating instead emotional scenarios around familial connections or self-realization. As postmodern theorist Jean Baudrillard argued, advertisers manipulate signs to tap into people's desires for prestige, power, or social bonding (1998).

In China, arenas that were once under strict state control have become thoroughly commodified since market reforms were implemented. Housing, gender identities, child rearing, and leisure time were once areas of life that the CCP sought to shape through a combination of socialist and Maoist ideology. Today, these are arenas that are portrayed, in advertisements and popular media, as subject to people's own control through the mechanisms of consumption. People in China increasingly expect to be able to shape these areas through the act of spending money.

A key question remains, however. Within Marx's original framework, consumers were portrayed as victims vis-à-vis corporations' commodification practices. Along similar lines, Baudrillard argued that shoppers have only an illusory sense of empowerment, and that in fact marketing and retailing techniques shape and direct their desires (1998: 79). Are consumers true decision makers, who can evaluate their choices and decide how to spend their resources? Or have corporations taken over the work of the CCP in organizing and manipulating behaviors in such domains as home life, child rearing, and gender expression? In this section, we will explore the commodification of these arenas of everyday life in China, and how corporations, through advertising, have shaped these domains and established new expectations, fantasies, and behaviors.

PRIVATE SPACE

The socialist era was characterized by not only the politicization of public spaces of work, consumption, and leisure, but also that of the traditionally private, domestic sphere (cf. Brownell 1995; Anagnost 1997; Rofel 1999). What were once privately owned homes and businesses became communal property. State officials assigned housing to families within their work units. Where one's home was, how it was furnished, and who one could live with were all subject to state supervision and intervention. By 1956, 95 percent of housing and land had been nationalized, as housing thus came under the redistributive economy. Local neighborhood watch leaders kept surveillance on people's activities within their homes, making sure they did not keep any artifacts that could betray a bourgeois background. Mao Zedong's portrait and other propaganda posters were the only forms of home décor that were allowed. Neighborhood snoops made sure their residents kept copies of Mao's *Little Red Book* on display, and did not own books that could be considered counter-revolutionary. Even areas as personal as courtship, women's reproductive systems, and children's upbringing were subject to the prying eyes and ears of the local work unit leaders, whose duty it was to ensure that their teams exhibited perfect revolutionary thought and action (Fraser 2000).

Under Deng Xiaoping's leadership, private home ownership gradually became legalized, as the government shifted its policies to encourage the growth of the domestic real estate market. Home owners bought the units they were already occupying, and new commercial developments started to pop up all over the urban landscape. Housing, like other arenas of life that were once strictly controlled by the state, became subject to the private sector. Homes were, once again, commodities, as opposed to parts of the collective. As demand began to outpace supply, prices have been driven up, particularly in the first-tier coastal cities such as Shanghai and Beijing. Concurrently, the state began to withdraw its heavy involvement in domestic life, leaving decisions around home décor, household finance management, and leisure time entertainment largely up to the families themselves.

Statistics on home ownership in China are somewhat inconclusive. The most optimistic numbers, put out by the People's Bank of China and the Southwestern University of Finance and Economics, state that nearly 90 percent of Chinese families own homes (2012). This compares with a world average of about 60 percent. Critics, however, question the methodology of the study, the representation in the sample size, and how "family" is defined. The study seems to lump adult children who still live with their parents as family, thus potentially skewing the percentage higher than it should be.

Despite the questionable statistics, home ownership is undoubtedly rising quickly in China. Homes are, like cars and other status items, associated with success and upward mobility. When we first met, Shen Yan was a 39-year-old real estate broker, who lived with his wife, son, and mother. He was also a proud home owner himself, and as we toured his home, he described his own journey towards home ownership.

> The home I am living in now was purchased on my own bit-by-bit via my diligence, hard work as well as some luck. In total it took me nine years from the moment I began to work until I moved into this new home. My home is related to my family's entire life, so it represents happiness. Buying a home means buying happiness for us Chinese.

Shen Yan went on to show me his four bedrooms – one for his mother, one for his wife, one for his son, and one as a study room. He went into great detail about the rosewood furniture and hardwood floors, which he felt exemplified his simple yet elegant taste. While his mother's room was fairly bare, the master bedroom was richly decorated with what he called "Elizabethan era" cushions and bedding. "The style of our home is sedate, which matches our personalities. We want our home to have a warm and harmonious atmosphere."

A large portrait of the couple and their son covered almost an entire wall. In the portrait, the couple is dressed in Western-style wedding attire, and the toddler is in a tuxedo. Curious about the timing of the photo, I asked if they had gotten married after having a child. Shen Yan explained that when they got married a decade ago, they could not afford professional wedding photos. A few years after the birth of their son and once his real estate practice took off, they decided to have them done. He then proceeded to pull out their wedding album and showed me various professionally shot photos of the couple in different outfits, including traditional Japanese and Chinese wedding attire.

We went on to visit the son's room. "It has all the amenities so that our kid has a relatively independent room. He has his own PC, and can study and read in here if he wants." Shen Yan emphasized how important it was to him to give his son this kind of privacy. "When I was growing up, we all shared one room and there was never a space that I could go to be by myself."

I asked Shen Yan to speak more about the importance of privacy, as neither traditional Chinese homes nor communal housing during Mao Zedong's regime had prioritized this as a value.

> The primary criterion in buying a home is to ensure everyone in a family has their own privacy and enough shared space for other activities, such as toilet, showering room, kitchen, dining room, living room, and balcony. If every member in the family has their own room, we can avoid conflict.

Since Shen Yan's mother lived with him, I asked whether or not he expected to live with his own son in the future.

> When I grow old, maybe I will live with my children. Or maybe not. The best way is to live in one building but on different floors. I would probably choose to live close to my children because it is necessary to communicate with each other to maintain the relationship with the family members. But, I do believe old people and their children need to have their own, independent room. I want to set an example to my children via my own behavior.

Shen Yan's home tour illustrated emerging values that consumers attach to their homes, as home ownership is rising in China. The first is this idea that home is a harmonious oasis for the family and an escape from the public world. In his exploration of the reintroduction of private housing in the 1990s, David Fraser traces the transformation of homes, which were once public, shared and multi-generational, into private, personal, and calming spaces (2000). During the Maoist years, homes were subject to constant monitoring in order to ensure proper behavior. Work units were structured in such a way that many of the activities that were formerly within the private domain – such as eating and bathing – were often relegated to shared, public facilities. The communal nature of the housing assignments ensured that there was very little that families could keep truly private.

The housing market today emphasizes radically different attributes. As Fraser observes, advertisements focus on the themes of respite and peace – what he calls the Oasification of housing (2000: 27). Home, now a commodity rather than part of the state's redistribution center, is reconfigured to be thought of as a haven, a calm escape from noisy, dirty, public urban spaces. In his role as a real estate agent, Shen Yan confirms that the most upscale housing complexes are those that look like they are far away from the hustle and bustle of the city. Rooftop gardens and other forms of greenery contribute to the idea of home as an oasis, a haven protected from public grime as well as the public gaze.

But it is not just retreating from the outside world that matters to families. It is also the ability to retreat from each other. Like Shen Yan, I have heard several other home owners emphasize the importance of having multiple rooms, so that everyone can have spaces of their own. As Shen Yan's home tour illustrated, it was also important to give each family member the ability to personalize their own space.

Related to changing values around the home are changing family structures. The One-Child Policy has resulted in smaller families. That, in correlation with higher income levels, means more space per person. In addition, the family is increasingly being defined as the nuclear family. While it is still common to see three generations under one roof, the expectation that a home should include the extended family is somewhat diminishing. What surprised me most in my research over the last few years is the increase in numbers of people who simply do not want to live with their adult children, and who envision a more independent lifestyle as retirees. Yao Hua Zhong, a 44-year-old IT manager, was frank about his desire not to live with his daughter when she is grown up. "The family members should have their own space to keep their privacy. When I get old, I won't live with my kids if I can afford another house. Everyone has their own style. I want to live according to my own style."

This notion of living "according to my own style" has also emerged as an outcome of the commodification of homes and home living. Furnishing companies such as IKEA have capitalized on the boom in real estate. The Swedish company has opened over a dozen stores in China, and its flagship store in Beijing sees more visitors every year than any other IKEA in the world. What appeals to consumers is not just the wide variety of furniture and household goods, but perhaps more importantly, the fantasies that IKEA encourages through creating visual vignettes of idealized home environments. Throngs of shoppers move through IKEA to learn about what their homes could look like. Yao Hua Zhong talks about creating a certain feel in his home.

> My home style is in a Nordic style. I decorate with modern art paintings and creative little things hanging on the wall. I purchase most things from IKEA and some from Taobao. These decorations give me a relaxed and cosy feeling. Home for me means safety, authenticity, relaxation, and love.

Indeed, home owners in China are playing with a mix of globally influenced styles. As we explored elsewhere, Western styles tend to denote the most status through their association with modernity. As homes have become privatized, they have become an alternative domain for status formation and self-expression. On the outskirts of the big cities are developments mimicking US suburban neighborhoods. About an hour outside Beijing's city center are gated subdivisions that originally sprung up to cater to expatriates. Today they are being built for the Chinese home buyer. Visually and architecturally, these suburbs have been modeled on the tract homes that have defined areas such as San Jose or Orange County in California. Their pastel colors, Spanish designs, manicured lawns, communal clubhouses, and golf courses mimic US suburban styles, and could not be any more different than the Chinese urban centers. Even the names of such developments conjure up distinctly un-Chinese images: Le Leman Lake, Capital Paradise, Yosemite, and River Garden (Elsea 2005).

Shanghai's "One City Nine Towns" project aimed to develop nine satellite cities, each with its own style mimicking a different European town. Thames Town, for example, mimics the architecture of an English town, with its Tudor mansions as well as its corner pubs and places to buy wine. The town also boasts a replica of Christ Church from Bristol, a popular backdrop for wedding photos, as well as a statue of Winston Churchill. No detail has been overlooked, as even the security guards of that development wear the red uniforms of Buckingham Palace. In Hangzhou, one development mimics Venice, with its manmade canals, style of architecture, and gondoliers. On the outskirts of Beijing is the Palais de Fortune development, which features French chateau style villas with materials imported from France (see Bosker 2013 for detailed analysis of architectural mimicry in China).

Such developments highlight how the commodification of housing has also spawned the commercialization of residential areas. Homes in China are increasingly being advertised in terms of their proximity to spaces of consumption. The clustering of facilities and services around luxury apartments reinforces the idea that home and its surroundings are consumption spaces. It can be difficult to see where shopping spaces end and living spaces begin. High-rise apartment dwellings often have commercial spaces on their ground floors, so that people can move from home space to shopping space simply by walking out of their front door. There is also a social currency in being close to five-star hotels and other spaces catering to people with wealth. It is as if by being close to them, people absorb the prestige associated with these places. In describing housing advertisements, which focus not just on the homes themselves but the commercial spaces around them, Fraser writes, "Each advertisement, to greater or lesser degree, constitutes a visual context for domestic life, a chart for the urban imagination. Each one is a panel of fantasy, within which is embedded the mosaic of commercialized dreams" (2000: 28).

RAISING CHILDREN

The raising of children is another area that has become subject to increased commodification over the last two decades. During the height of Mao Zedong's reign, children held a special place in Chinese society as the new generation of revolutionaries. Mao called upon the youth to demonstrate proper behavior to their own parents, who may have been harboring bourgeois tendencies. During the Cultural Revolution, youths were called upon to join the Red Guard and travel the country to extol Mao's teachings. Traditional, Confucian hierarchies were disrupted, as the young were encouraged to overthrow their elders and take on the leadership of Mao Zedong's revolution.

Today, children can similarly be considered as at the forefront of China's consumer revolution. This is most evident in the fact that children are now seen as a market segment of their own by corporations, who bring in experts on infant, toddler, and youth culture, and who regularly conduct consumer research among even the youngest Chinese. TV commercials, online ads, and colorful packaging speak directly to children, often bypassing the parents in their attempt to foster a desiring young segment. Consumption spaces are often designed with the very young consumer in mind, with bright and tantalizing play spaces, cheerful mascots, and special freebies such as toys. Casual dining areas entice young visitors with their advertisements of festive birthday parties, complete with balloons and trinkets. Within the hypermarkets, prime shelving space is dedicated to children's foods, which promise brighter, stronger, happier children to parents. It is not unusual to see children leading the way when grocery shopping, drawing parents towards the aisles where happy, smiling young faces adorn boxes of biscuits or yogurt containers.

Chinese parents are, likewise, being inundated with advertisements and other persuasive forms of corporate messaging that make them hyper-aware of the connection between consumption and good parenthood. As marketing specialist and parent Chris Liu lamented, corporations get to parents by emphasizing the saying, "Don't let your kids lose at the starting point." From the birth of their children, parents in China are pressured by society and corporate marketing to give their little emperor or empress the very best money can buy. Early Childhood Education Centers target children five years and under, and focus on mental and physical exercises to help children get ready for school, career, and life. For school-aged children, private after-school and weekend classes are becoming a norm, as pressure mounts to do well at every stage along the way in order eventually to reach the best universities, and then graduate into the best careers. Those who "only" go to regular, mandated classes during the day are considered at a disadvantage. In addition to core subjects such as math and foreign languages, children are also being sent to private art, music, and sports classes, for the sake of preparing them to be exceptional in the future. The pressure is especially high on China's males, for it is a well-known fact that males outnumber females. Only the most successful males will find good wives, so the logic goes.

Because of the rapidly transforming norms, parents are sometimes at a loss for what they should do. Their own parents grew up so differently that they do not feel as if they can look to them as models. New parents thus often look to peer support networks for mentorship to figure out what "good" parenthood is in the context of consumption. Li Jue, a young mother who doted nonstop on her chubby, 18-month-old boy, talked about the importance of her social networking groups in her childrearing practices.

> I have a QQ Mother's Group that I check in with every day when my baby is sleeping. I go there to share ideas about what foods to buy. I ask their opinions about things I see online. I share my experience with different baby products. Just the other day, one of the mothers shared her opinion about the new baby spas opening up in the city. They provide special baths for babies in a spring time temperature, so babies can stay healthy and breathe well, and not get sick from all the dry winter air. These are so popular, you have to book weeks in advance to get your baby an appointment. But because of her recommendation, I will look into it.

In the quest to give their children the best that money can buy, parents are increasingly inundated with messages that equate science and modernity with product superiority. The boom in yogurt products for children over the last decade is in no small part related to successful advertising linking milk products to increased health and intelligence. Brands such as Heinz, that make products geared towards children, include English in their packaging in China, in order to emphasize the association between the West and science. As Jun Jing, whose work focuses on children and food notes, "Selling the Heinz rice product along with a dose of science and modernity has a special appeal in a society where the urban family's priority in spending its disposable income is its single child" (2000: 19).

In a research project I conducted on perceptions of Western fast-food restaurants, the parents I interviewed in Beijing and Shanghai described the food as clean, nutritious, and made with the most scientifically advanced methods. Part of this is the association with the West and modernity – fast-food places such as KFC and McDonald's embody the new and modern. But part of this is also how the fast-food restaurants themselves advertise their offerings. While in the West fast food is typically advertised in terms of low prices, in China, there is an emphasis on the proven nutritious aspects of the food. I frequently heard parents refer to the milk and bread products in Western restaurants as having more *yinyang* (nutrition) than Chinese snacks, and thus being not just acceptable but desirable substitutes for home-cooked meals.

This association between science and product brands can sometimes blur the lines between product advertising and objective information dissemination. Ji Ying Jiang, a new father with an infant son, related his experience with the company Pfizer, which makes Wyeth milk powder.

> At about 4:00 p.m., I finally got through to the special childrearing line provided by Wyeth Milk Powder and asked some questions concerning the growth of babies and the problems my baby was encountering. I got professional answers. But I had to wait for a long time because there were so many callers, and the time I got with the expert was limited. I wish I could have asked more questions. The expert suggested that since our baby is being breastfed, that I buy some pistachios and walnuts for my wife to eat. They also suggested some specific branded products that would be good for our baby. I called the Wyeth hotline again when my baby had a runny nose and got some good suggestions. I ended up buying what she suggested to help my baby breathe better.

The desire to ensure their children have the best future money can buy has even created a market for "birth tourism." Mainland Chinese women who have the financial resources pay for the privilege to travel to Hong Kong and give birth to their children there. When a child is born in Hong Kong, he or she automatically receives Hong Kong residency. This has become such a popular practice that native Hong Kong residents have complained about the shortage of hospital facilities due to the influx of pregnant women from Mainland China. A growing number of pregnant Chinese women are also flying to the USA to give birth. Women are provided nursing staff, meals, and a nursery. The entire package, including travel, visas, and other expenses, runs to about $25,000. The mothers typically return to China with their babies, with the expectation that as US citizens, their children can return when they are older to take advantage of the benefits of citizenship. As Aihwa Ong argues in her work on transnational Chinese practices, the ability to secure such forms of "flexible citizenship" is among the ultimate markers of status and success (1999).

GENDER

The Shanghai Propaganda Poster Art Center features a collection of prints from the 1950s to 1970s. While once covering the walls of nearly all public places, today they are collected in this space as a form of art and a nostalgic reminder of the past. Happy faces beam from these posters, which portray heroic workers in utopian communities, students as Red Guards, and Mao Zedong himself, glorious and god-like. What I found most striking from the point of view of Chinese society today are the portrayals of women. Sturdy, robust, and sometimes as big and burly as men, they look very different from the women in today's cosmetics and fashion advertisements. As the consumer revolution has progressed over the last few decades, women's beauty, sexuality, and expressions of gender have become dramatically commoditized.

What it meant to be a woman was, throughout the decades of Mao Zedong's rule, a highly politicized and public topic. He declared that old forms of femininity, including long hair, make-up, high heels, and skirts, created gendered, unequal citizens. He went as far as to argue that these traditional expressions of the feminine marked women as criminals – shackled and punished (Otis 2012: 17). To combat this, the CCP prescribed a unisex look for everyone – short hair, baggy pants, and shapeless jackets. Women's worth was defined through their participation in nation building, in which they were to be seen as equal members of the labor force. Thus in early propaganda posters, women's bodies were portrayed as similar to men's in terms of build, communicating strength and the ability to do any form of manual labor. Women's clothing and appearances were strictly controlled in order to erase differences between the genders. Sexuality was muted, and the CCP discouraged predominant norms around femininity in order to challenge traditional gender dichotomies, which were deemed bourgeois in spirit and counter-revolutionary.

Xiao Xiao, the 54-year-old retiree we met in an earlier chapter, recounted the changes in how women adorned themselves.

> During the Cultural Revolution we were not allowed to wear colorful shirts or bell-bottomed pants. We couldn't perm our hair or wear miniskirts and high heels. We were all uniform, in order to show respect for the revolution. Great changes have been taking place. Today we can wear novel clothing in various styles. So many different brands have emerged, giving us endless ways to pursue personalization.

This theme of personalization comes up in other interviews around women's changing roles in society. Xie Yan Zuo, the 21-year-old Jeep fan, talked about her perception of change over time.

> Personalization is something that my parents and grandmother didn't have. They were born in the old society without freedom. Women could not go out casually and their marriages were arranged, they also needed

to wrap their feet tightly in order to let the feet look smaller. I can manage my economy by myself, be independent, free, decide on who I want to marry, and be equal to men.

Like other young, professional women, Xie Yan Zuo talked about freedom of expression through physical adornment. Not being forced to bind her feet, being able to choose from different clothing styles, and having the right to decide her own future are all interrelated aspects of the transformation of women's roles. She went on to say: "These days, young women can go to the stores and decide on what they want to look like. They can look professional or like a cute Japanese manga girl. They can look natural or like a *linglei* (punk). It is our own choice now."

Women's increased sense of autonomy from both the state and traditional expectations is frequently articulated in terms of their choices as consumers. Didier Perot-Minot, Senior Marketing Manager at Sephora China, has observed that cosmetics and fashion are important vehicles for Chinese women to differentiate themselves in an era that prioritizes individualism over the collective. Within the Sephora stores, women come in and experiment not just with make-up but with new identities. Because Sephora represents a democratic shopping experience, in which anyone can come in, wander, and be free to try on new things, young women with limited incomes can also participate in the quest for self-expression through make-up.

Gyms, yoga studios, and other kinds of health clubs have become popular over the last decade. The idea of physical exercise in a place where you pay is very new to China, but has become associated with an upwardly mobile lifestyle. But women are not the only ones interested in physical health and setting themselves apart by their figures. Men are also joining gyms in record numbers. For some, it is to lose weight, as attention to figures is not limited to women. Overweight employees are often considered lazy and unattractive, and unlike in the USA, remarks about physicality from colleagues or even managers are not discouraged. Foreigners who become friends with locals in China are often surprised by how direct these comments can be.

In addition to the internet, traditional magazines also play important roles in the exploration of womanhood and manhood in the context of consumer culture. Bookstores are typically crowded with young people browsing the magazine racks. City corners and malls feature magazine stands with an ever-growing variety of titles. When economic reforms began in 1978, the only magazines widely available contained political propaganda. In the early 1990s, the first fashion magazine, appropriate called *Trends*, made its debut. Today, there are hundreds of titles across business, fashion, food, technology, fitness, and travel. Some fashion magazines, like *Cosmopolitan*, have started splitting their monthly issue into two magazines because they became too thick to print. Hearst, which publishes *Elle*, has even designed plastic and cloth bags for women to easily carry these heavy magazines home.

Feng Sha Chen, a 41-year-old CFO in a multi-national corporation, described the role of magazines in her own journey as a woman.

> *Elle* is the first magazine about fashion and female topics that came to China. I first read *Elle* twenty years ago. The magazine has influenced a whole generation. It taught us about Western fashion and lifestyles. The articles encouraged women to be independent, sexy, and elegant. I not only learned about luxury goods, but also about sexual satisfaction. This magazine helps not only in fashion but in psychological health.

While the first wave of lifestyle magazines targeted women, publications focused on men's health, fashion, and sports are among the fastest growing titles. Like women's magazines, they play important roles in men's explorations of their own gender identities, sexuality, and success. *FHM* and *Maxim* show scantily clad Asian women, while *Men's Health*, *Men's Box*, and *Men's Style* appear to appeal to mixed gay and straight audiences. The fragile scholar of traditional China and the plain worker celebrated under Maoism have made way to muscular, tanned bodies sporting European suits, Cartier watches, and hair gel. Like the female body, the male body has become a site for a new kind of self-expression, reinforced by consumerism.

While both women and men in China experience greater autonomy in terms of self-expression, career development, and family choices, they also face other challenges related to the commoditization of beauty and desire. Having lived and worked in China for over twenty years, I am most surprised at the reversal of the gender neutrality that Mao Zedong championed. Women, in particular, are inundated with images that celebrate the hyper-feminine and sexualized (Honig and Hershatter 1988). Long gone are the posters featuring women laboring equally alongside men. They have been replaced with advertisements featuring slimming products, skin whitening creams, and other images that mark women as distinct, different, and successful because of their feminine physicality. While gender inequalities continued to exist under Mao, the overarching public message was that women could do anything men could do and "hold up half the sky." Today, women continue to express narratives around equality, but increasingly, they emphasize their looks as pivotal to their own success. In my interviews with younger women, I am sometimes surprised by the emphasis on physicality. One young woman from Shanghai was very frank about the topic:

> To keep young and beautiful forever is the dream of all women. I'm no exception. Women only want to make themselves more beautiful and more elegant and live a pleasant life. They care about nothing else. If you are ugly, you will not get a good office job. And you will not find a rich husband.

The search for rich husbands has spawned its own forms of commoditization. The "De Yu Nu Zi" school, which means "moral education for women," opened in 2010 in Beijing, and promises to teach women how to catch their own successful male. For about US$1,000, students are given courses with titles such as "whom you should marry," "tame your husband," and "read his mind." Some courses deal frankly with the issue of handling men's roving eyes and what to do if they are caught having affairs. Reality dating TV shows have emerged in recent years, capturing millions of viewers with their young, slender, outspoken female contestants looking for financially well-off suitors.

The economic boom has also led to the rise in sexual commodification. Many different forms have arisen in China. On one end of the spectrum is what would be considered straightforward prostitution. Women solicit customers in mid to low-end hotels or work in massage parlors that offer more than just the standard massage. In the middle of the spectrum are escort girls, who work as bar or KTV hostesses. They are not required to offer sexual services, but can choose to do so for their favorite customers. On the other end of the spectrum are women who become mistresses or second wives to rich men. These may develop as implicit or explicit arrangements, with actual contracts, time frames, and amounts agreed upon in advance. The practice of becoming mistresses is not new to this current era. In fact, the term for mistress, *ernai*, harks back to the polygamous traditions of pre-Maoist China. As it is today, keeping mistresses on the side was a sign of a man's financial success. One particular dating website, called *Baoyang*, which means to provide financial support for someone of the opposite sex, matches young, single women and married men. The posts from men often include monthly "salaries" and other benefits including furnished apartments and luxury sports cars.

The motivations of these women, however, can be complex, and go beyond the preference to be in the back seat of a BMW as opposed to the back of a bicycle. During the late 1990s, I befriended a woman named Chen Yi. She had just earned a degree in dermatology and hoped to develop a line of her own facial products based on indigenous Chinese herbs. When we first met, she was a single mother of an 8-year-old daughter. Years later, when we reconnected, she mentioned in passing she had a husband, but was vague about their relationship and I noticed he was never around. She finally revealed to me that he was an entrepreneur from Taiwan, who had opened up a shoe factory in Fujian province. He had a wife and family back in Taiwan, but because he came to China often, he also sought out a second wife there. She not only became his lover, but also his business partner. His trust in her was so high that much of his business was registered under her name. Today, she is the managing director of his enterprise, overseeing shipments of products around the world. Their relationship, she tells me, is still close, but they are not lovers anymore. He has moved on to a younger mistress, and she remains his closest business confidante. She has sent her daughter to study in the USA, and lives with her maid in an upscale, suburban complex. Chen Yi's case illustrates the complexity of the role of mistresses. While on the one hand they demonstrate the commodification of women's sexuality, on the other hand, we see that some women use these opportunities to develop their own careers.

HOLIDAYS AND CELEBRATIONS

Marcel Mauss's classic work, *The Gift*, examines what gift giving can illuminate in terms of human relationships. He argues that gifts are never "free," but rather, lead to reciprocal exchange. Gifts are, in Mauss's terms, imbued with "spiritual mechanisms" that engage the honor of both giver and receiver. The giver not only gifts an object, but part of himself: "the objects are never completely separated from the men who exchange them" (1990: 31). Thus, the act of giving creates not just an obligation but also a social bond. Mauss's work recast gifts as symbols of human relationships.

Gift giving during the decades under Mao Zedong was fairly modest and largely dictated by local officials. Gifts for newly married couples or new parents were typically arranged by the work units, and included practical goods such as a new quilt or a bicycle for the family to use. Neighbors and friends would pool together their meager savings and purchase a bag of peanuts – considered a luxurious item at the time.

In recent years, however, gift giving has become thoroughly subject to the conspicuous spending that characterizes China's consumer culture. Much of this is related to the introduction of Western holidays, such as Valentine's Day and Christmas. These occasions were virtually non-existent in China just a few decades ago, but have become major commercial events (Watson 2000). Shopping areas are transformed in late November into winter wonderlands, with festive decorations, twinkling lights, and Santa displays. Stores blast Christmas music, while big malls celebrate with tree lighting ceremonies. Swimming pools are converted into ice-skating rinks. Consumers in China have, nonetheless, localized this global holiday. While in the West it still holds some religious significance and is generally thought of as a time for family, in China, Christmas is a time to celebrate with friends outside the home. Shopping sprees and eating out with big groups of friends and colleagues have become established ways of celebrating the holiday. High-end hotels and restaurants offer Christmas buffets, featuring a mix of Asian and Western dishes, and hypermarkets carry Christmas themed sweets.

Likewise, Valentine's Day has become a major gift giving occasion among couples, as the idea of romance becomes increasingly commoditized. During the Maoist years, the relationship between men and women was framed as one of comrades and partners in the socialist revolution. Romance was downplayed as a sign of materialistic, bourgeois thinking. In the last decade, romance has become a much more talked about and explored aspect of relationships, no doubt bolstered by advertisements linking specific products to enhanced relationships between couples. China is now the world's second-largest diamond jewelry market after the USA, with demand growing as couples seek to demonstrate their commitment to each other through the new practice of giving and wearing engagement rings. Five-star hotels offer Valentine's Day packages for couples, featuring couples spa retreats and romantic dinners with European wines.

Weddings have also become thoroughly commercialized in China over the last few decades. Five-star hotels offer elaborate banquet celebrations with all of the trimmings. Brides-to-be can shop for Western style white wedding dresses at the Vera Wang store in Shanghai, or buy knock-off Very Wang gowns on Taobao. Travel agencies are marketing destinations such as Hainan Island, the Maldives, and Hawaii as honeymoon locations. As we saw in Shen Yan's home tour earlier in this chapter, professional photos featuring newlyweds (or older couples) posing in a variety of wedding outfits from around the world, with backdrops such as Christ Church in Thames Town, have become important signs marking a couple's relationship. As Miller et al. put it, "Social relations have become more rather than less dense, and maintaining these relations in turn demands constant and considerable consumer expenditure" (1998: 17). The social media website Renren. com estimated that weddings can cost up to US$200,000 in China's big cities.

Yun Yue, the self-described *xiaozi* we met in the chapter on Lifestyles, described the effect her friend's wedding had on her own aspirations.

> The MC started off by reading a fairy tale about a little angel who became a beautiful bride and came to the wishing tree to look for her prince charming. Then the couple came out. The most memorable moment was when they exchanged wedding rings. A small toy helicopter flew over them slowly and delivered the ring to the bridegroom. It

was romantic and surprising, like a fairy tale. After seeing this wedding ceremony, it made me look forward to my own wedding party some day.

Birthdays, especially for children, have also become increasingly subject to commercialization within the last few decades. Traditionally, only the birthdays of infants and the elderly were celebrated. Today, children's birthdays have become a big business for Western fast-food restaurants, bowling alleys, and children's amusement parks. Children in China have learned through the media and their peers to demand birthdays with party favors, cakes, and gifts. As one parent put it, "Throwing a big birthday party shows that my child is special."

EATING THE OTHER

In an earlier chapter, we explored the role of travel in defining emerging consumer lifestyles. While the primary interest is in foreign locations, particularly those that signify modernity and luxury, in recent years, I have also observed a growing desire to experience the "exotic" within China. These are places that had, up until recently, been mostly derided as backward and of little interest because they were less modernized than the cities. Feminist writer bell hooks (Gloria Jean Watkins) refers to cultural commodification as "eating the other" (1994). By this she means that the dominant culture engages in buying or acquiring a piece of the "primitive." The cultures of minorities, poor, or other marginal communities thus become commercialized for the enjoyment of others, primarily through tourism.

Some comments from a study I conducted on travel revealed a fascination with China's most extreme regions:

"I want to visit Tibet and buy precious medicinal herbs only found there."

"I want to feel close to nature when I travel. I want to go to Tibet, Xinjiang, and Hainan. These places are the last places in China that are unpolluted. I want to feel the charm of nature that will set my spirit free."

"I want to go to Xishuangbanna (in Yunnan province) and Hainan Island. These are like fairylands in my imagination, and I want to see if they are really like that."

"I hope there are surprises in my life often to make life more interesting. Inner Mongolia. At the grassland. It is a place I can speak loudly."

Tibet, Inner Mongolia, Xinjiang, and Hainan – what these places have in common is that for urban residents from the first-tier cities, they represent "exotic" China. They are known for their ethnic minorities and "simpler," "traditional" lifestyles. The majority Han ethnic group tends to view these minorities as quaint and less touched by economic development. In desiring to visit these places, urban Chinese are seeking out a sense of authenticity that they believe is missing from their current lifestyles. They mention motivations like getting away from the polluted cities, discovering local customs, and feeling closer to nature.

In his ethnographic work in the northwestern city of Anshan, Michael Griffiths highlights urban middle-class fascination with rural life. The desire to experience the natural, easygoing, and traditional countryside has spawned a tourist industry in poor rural areas. Savvy farmers have transformed their peasant homes into tourist destinations, as they provide beds and food for weekend visitors from the cities. Some, Griffiths notes, have even gotten rich from this urban interest in the rural lifestyle, and end up disguising their own wealth in order to keep up the appearance of a "simple" rural lifestyle. Coarse grain, or the unrefined rice that is typical of rural areas, has actually become a food trend among urbanites. Unlike the bleached white rice that characterizes urban, middle-class lifestyles, coarse grain has come to stand for chemical-free, natural food. Restaurants in cities such as Anshan are even capitalizing on the interest in eating the other, both literally and figuratively, by offering dishes, such as coarse grain, that evoke the countryside (2013).

In their search for the authentic in the rural countryside or in "exotic," faraway places such as Tibet, Chinese travelers are not just seeking to consume products, but also to consume experiences. On the one hand, travel can bring people closer to the modern lifestyles they seek out, through luxury brand shopping or experiencing cosmopolitan lifestyles. On the other hand, travel can validate their own modern lifestyles through the commercialized versions of traditional, marginal, or exotic culture. Rural, folk, and ethnic China become consumption objects for urban lifestyles (Lefebvre 1996; Schein 2000).

THEORETICAL CONSIDERATIONS

Under Mao Zedong's rule, everyday life in China came to be shaped by political ideology. What people ate, wore, did for a living, and enjoyed during their time off all became subject to state control and public censure. Everything from the décor of one's home to the length of a woman's hair and how she adorned herself were pronounced as signs of political ideology. Thus, conforming to state sanctioned norms around how to conduct one's self in domestic as well as public life became important in order to avoid punishment. In the last three decades, however, these areas of life that were once shaped by political ideology have now come under the influence of the market. Home-making, child rearing, gender expressions, celebrations, and urban–rural relations are becoming increasingly subject to the forces of commodification. In each of these arenas, people are no longer subject to the CCP's ideological expectations, but rather, to new forms of authority represented by producers. What it means to be a good parent or a successful woman are thus becoming increasing defined by what one purchases to address specific concerns. It can be argued the major influence on everyday lifestyles is now a consumerist ideology.

From a theoretical perspective, this chapter touches upon a key question within the consumption literature. What drives consumer culture – is it the producers, who develop goods and create needs through advertising and branding, and then satisfy those needs with their products? Or is it the consumers, who have needs in the first place, and then fulfill these needs through their choice of what to acquire? One common and widespread critique of the classical theories around consumption, particularly those deriving from Marx, is that they privilege production, portraying consumption largely in terms of people's passive submission to what corporations put in front of them. Such critiques have merit in the sense that Marx and other influential early observers of industrial capitalism, including Max Weber and Georg Simmel, were concerned primarily with the systems of capitalism and the economic aspects of work. Early consumption studies evolved out of the economic/Marxian view that inherently sees consumers as alienated beings, somehow tricked into buying things through the greedy producers, who trick them into thinking the only way to fulfill their needs is to buy their products. Adorno and Horkheimer (2000) furthered the Marxian dismissal of consumers, arguing that employers' need for objectified and submissive workers created a parallel need for dominated, passive consumers. They described consumer culture as soothing and entertaining but ultimately banal, and the antithesis of the creativity that marked the artisanal economy.

While several other chapters in this book explore consumer agency and the increased freedoms people have to express themselves, this chapter balances out that perspective by exploring how consumers are simultaneously experiencing constraint due to the agendas of corporations. This chapter also serves as a caution against taking an overly celebratory view about China's consumer revolution, which is common in the business and popular literature. As we have seen, consumers in China are increasingly influenced by how producers frame certain ideals around being good parents or attractive men or women. The hyper-attention to women's physical beauty and the materially based expectations that pervade relationships have created new structures within which individuals must operate. Likewise, parents' perceptions of healthy, happy children are being shaped by children's food and product makers, who conveniently offer the right solutions.

What we see in China is that the process of commodification and the increased role of consumption in even the most private areas of people's lives have created a complex mix of new freedoms and new constraints. Nonetheless, consumers in China are neither always in a state of exploitation nor are they always in a state of liberation. They occupy gray areas between the two extremes, moving back and forth along the spectrum from context to context. To argue that they are all victims of capitalism's agendas is to miss the ways in which individuals shape their daily lives and future aspirations through the use of money for goods and services. To argue that they are entirely able to shape their own lives is to miss the ways in which producers have, to a large degree, replaced the role of the state in setting forth ideologies about the "right" way to live.

The commodification of an increasing proportion of everyday life is, nonetheless, of concern to a growing number of Chinese citizens. The next chapter explores the ways in which people speak out about their rights as consumers as well as citizens, and seek to push back on both corporations as well as the state in certain circumstances.

6 | Awareness

Yin Feng was a 28-year-old who spent all of his non-working and non-sleeping time engaging in online gaming. His entire social life revolved around a community of gamers, who played with each other online as well as posted their thoughts about gaming trends in online forums and microblogs. His room was his entire world, and his set-up included two large screens, a high-end audio system, several keyboards, and, on the walls, posters of female Japanese pop stars in seductive outfits and manga characters. In addition to what he acknowledged was a gaming "addiction," Yin Feng was also an avid microblogger. He posted several times a day, commenting on stories as far ranging as new PC games to the best place to get Taiwanese style beef noodles in Shanghai. He followed hundreds of people, many of them what he called serious microbloggers, who posted news items that were not covered in the official media. Despite the fact that he often seemed disconnected to the world outside his room because of his obsession with gaming, he was actually very concerned about what was happening in China due to rapid economic development.

> People see the wounded or the helpless on the street and they don't do anything to help. There are more and more cases in which people break off their old friendships and pretend not to know old friends when they are in need. There are too many property disputes among family members. A lot of young people have become depressed and cold and accept this reality as if there is nothing they can do to change the

current condition of society. Family relationships, love, friendship, ambition, faith, and conscience are being corroded gradually by this distorted value system.

I asked him what he thought the reasons were behind these negative changes.

> Nowadays, everyone is getting richer, more advanced, and more open in their outlook. We have achieved great success by challenging ourselves. However, we have not developed our moral conditions and social relationships in the same way. The morality base line is getting lower and lower. The ecological and cultural environments are getting worse. And there will be no improvement in the short term. Materialism is contaminating the entire society. This generation has already been greatly impacted, so what about the next generation?

The consumer revolution in China is typically framed in terms of how it has allowed people more opportunities for self-fulfillment, developing social status, and realizing aspirations. Nonetheless, consumers in China are also deeply aware of the consequences of increased production and consumption on their environment, moral order, and health. In his narrative, Yin Feng argues that moral and social development has not kept pace with economic development. While some articulate their despair and sense that these negative consequences of consumption are beyond their own control, others have taken to activism in various forms. The most widespread and remarkable has been the use of the internet as a way of sharing news and ideas about social, economic, and environmental issues. While members of China's younger generation are often blamed by their elders for being self-centered and materialistic, they are nonetheless at the forefront of new communities of activism that seek to spread information and get people involved in becoming smarter and more influential consumers.

This chapter explores the growing awareness among consumers in China of their role as active agents in shaping their own contexts and desired futures. While consumption is often framed in terms of the self or immediate family, this chapter explores how people in China are thinking about society-wide consequences, and the part they can play in instituting positive change. The topic of social activism in China is immense and complex, due to ever-changing governmental levels of tolerance for dissent and free speech. In this chapter, I will approach the topic from the perspective of consumption, and how individuals seek to participate in society-wide change through their specific roles as consumers.

MORALITY

In 2011, the nation was rocked by video footage showing a toddler being run over by a car, ignored by over a dozen people passing by, and run over a second time by another driver. The footage shows people clearly noticing the bleeding 2-year-old and motorists swerving to avoid her body, but nobody stopping to help. An elderly woman passing by eventually pulled the child to the side of the road, but the toddler had sustained such trauma that she eventually died in the hospital. The video footage, taken from a nearby security camera, went viral on the internet, and sparked a nationwide conversation about the state of Chinese morality.

Commentators attributed the coldness of the passers-by to a variety of reasons. One is the pervasive fear people have in China of getting involved with strangers. In another well-known case, a 65-year-old woman fell and broke her hip while attempting to board a bus in Nanjing. A man helped her up, gave her 200 *renminbi*, and escorted her to the hospital, staying until her family arrived. In return, he was sued for being the one who knocked her down, despite the lack of any evidence. Such incidents have made people wary of helping others, for fear of any misunderstandings that could end up as lawsuits. The low trust in the fairness of the legal system exacerbates the apprehension with getting involved in the affairs of strangers.

A second line of reasoning, however, links such incidents to rapid economic development. Moral development has not kept pace with economic development, people lament. Social commentators in the media argue that consumer culture has contributed to self-centeredness and the decay of "traditional" Chinese values. One mother and elementary school teacher in Shanghai described an idealized past that is being supplanted.

> The current moral or spiritual state of China is declining. People used to be honest and simple. They used to stick to traditional culture. They used to be self-disciplined. Now people only focus on money. They don't respect traditional culture. There are fewer illiterates now but the moral state hasn't improved. People are cold and selfish.

Similarly, Yin Feng, the online gamer, argued that China's cultural foundation is being threatened by its economic development.

> I don't think the moral state of China today is satisfying. But people need guidance from the media and our leadership. It seems that we are sacrificing our cultural foundation for economic development. Of course it is not an issue only in China. Some Western countries also had the same problem during their initial development. We should go back to our traditional values. We should promote the construction of a moral society even as we develop into a modern nation.

When people talk about tradition or losing tradition, I often press them to say more about what they mean by the term tradition. In their narratives, they always skip over the period of socialist reform under Mao Zedong, as if it had not happened, and talk as if China's traditions were consistently practiced until extreme materialism got in the way in the last decade or two. They thus envision a continuous Chinese cultural lineage, only recently interrupted. In Lisa Rofel's work on Chinese women's constructions of the past, she argues that her informants engage in a form of "structured forgetting" when developing their own life narratives (1999). I have observed a similar phenomenon, as people construct the present as a time of turmoil and moral decay, and a vaguely defined "past" as a time when tradition was intact.

The root of this moral decay is also attributed to a blind worship of all things foreign. Yin Feng, the online gamer, spoke of the perils of becoming too enamored with the West.

> When we absorb many Western cultures, there appears a kind of blindness, and even a kind of extremism. We think all foreign cultures are good so we absorb it all and do not digest properly. Being too admiring of foreign cultures produces all kind of problems. Young people would rather celebrate foreign holidays like Christmas and Valentine's Day, ignoring traditional festivals. They don't like folk music but have a fever for rock, rap, and other Western pop music. It is undeniable that we have the poorest understanding towards our traditional cultures than in any other period in our history.

Yin Feng's perspective reflects a niche yet growing sentiment, a counterpoint to the desire for extreme cosmopolitanism that was explored in an earlier chapter.

At 28, Yin Feng is a relatively young critic of China's consumer patterns. I have found that it is typically not the older generation of those who remember the frugal years under Mao Zedong's rule that are the biggest critics of consumer culture. Rather, those who are in the sort of "middle" generation, born in the 1970s and 1980s, who are especially critical of China's youth. Mu Mu, a 32-year-old HR director, expressed her frustration over China's young adult generation.

Those born since the 1990s are extremely self-centered and selfish. The one-child generation faces a mountain of pressure because of the 4-2-1 phenomenon. They enjoy perfect love from their parents and grandparents and have become selfish and self-oriented. They don't know hardship. When facing significant events or pressure, their bearing is not strong. They become timid, afraid of working too hard and suffering. It seems that they can't assume responsibility at all. Lack of responsibility is the biggest problem.

On the other end of the spectrum in terms of age and experience, are the political elite, who have been criticized broadly for their lavish ways and corrupt practices. Despite state attempts to monitor and control online content, microbloggers exposed graft among political officials, accusing them of spending state funds on luxury goods, vacations, and even their mistresses. Netizens have made sure the online public knows which leaders are sporting expensive watches and driving sports cars. This practice has fueled public outrage over the lifestyles of the political elite, in light of the mass poverty and social issues that plague so much of the rest of China. Throughout early 2013, the media regularly featured stories of officials owning hundreds of properties, fleeing abroad with bribes, or photographed at work with luxury accessories.

In March of 2013, China's new president and premier, Xi Jinping, pledged at the National People's Congress that his government would "resolutely reject formalism, bureaucratism, hedonism, and extravagance, and resolutely fight against corruption and other misconduct in all manifestations." He declared that the state would cut official spending on banquets, foreign trips, and cars, as well as reduce the government payroll. Chinese radio and television stations were instructed to ban advertisements for luxury items, as part of the governmental push to discourage extravagance and waste. This has had a drastic effect on the sale of luxury goods. Products such as expensive liquors, a banquet staple for senior officials, took a nosedive at the beginning of 2013. Heeding the public's general mood, the officials who showed up at the National People's Congress displayed much less of their typical osten-tatious show of expensive cars and fashion.

PATRIOTISM

A dispute between China and Japan over a group of uninhabited islands led to a consumer uprising in 2012. Known as Senkaku in Japan and Diaoyu in China, the islands boast rich fishing grounds and potential oil reserves. Perhaps most importantly, the islands occupy a strategic location between China, Japan, and Taiwan. In September 2012, the Japanese government purchased the remaining three of the disputed islands that it did not already own from their private owner. This prompted heated words from Beijing, which threatened military conflict. The international conflict also erupted on the streets of China, as angry Chinese protested in front of Japanese-owned businesses, boycotted Japanese goods, and smashed the windows of Japanese autos. Anger among the Chinese population had a noticeable effect on sales, with Japanese automakers reporting close to 10 percent drops in sales in China during the last part of 2012. All Nippon Airways, Japan's largest airline, reported fifty thousand cancellations of flights between the two countries in the same time frame. Retailers who featured Japanese products in their stores were pressured to take those products down or face the wrath of anti-Japan protestors. A number of Japanese companies and factories, including Panasonic, Honda, and Toyota, suspended their operations temporarily, amid the demonstrations.

Underlying this outbreak is a long history of anti-Japanese senti-ment in China. It has its roots in the Japanese invasion of China in 1937, which Chinese historians allege led to the mass killings and rapes of what has come to be known as the Nanjing Massacre. The continued animosity also stems from a national envy around Japan's role as the first Asian nation to become a world power. When the Japanese are brought up in terms of such historical relationships, the response is immediate and unequivocal – people say they "hate" the Japanese. But on an everyday basis, perceptions of Japan are much more balanced. Fascination with Japanese pop culture, cuisine, fashion, music, and trends counterbalance this "hatred." I have seen in my own research an almost cognitive dissonance when it comes to Japan. People pay lip service to their hatred of the nation, yet they are enamored with the culture. This interest in the culture is strongest with the younger generations, who may have been less inundated with anti-Japanese history in their education, and who have more extensive ties with Japan through the internet, and thus judge the culture based on more than their history books.

Yet when the Chinese state indicated that it had been provoked by Japan, Chinese citizens emphasized hatred over fascination. By focusing their protest around the destruction of and boycott of Japanese products, they conflated their roles as patriots with their roles as consumers. The space of consumption thus became their protest platform, a form of "consumer nationalism" (Garon and Maclachlan 2006: 10). Japan, in turn, felt the weight of Chinese protest in terms of its product sales.

Feng Sha Chen, the 41-year-old female CFO we met earlier, put it this way:

> During the tense period between China and Japan, boycotting Japanese goods became one of the most direct ways to express our anger. Japan is an island of phobia, with leaders that keep their old, narrow thinking. The world is round and everyone has countless ties and connections with others. However, Japan has gone too far this time. By boycotting Japanese goods, we can let the Japanese know that they must not trifle

with the Chinese. Now Japan has witnessed China's tough attitude. We can bring economic disaster on them.

This boycott of Japanese goods in 2012 was not an isolated event. The 2008 Beijing Olympics was to be China's coming out to the world, proof that it deserved to be a superpower. However, the grand spectacle was not without controversy or critics. As the Olympic torch passed through Paris, protestors against China's occupation of Tibet blocked the torch-bearer and attempted to wrestle the torch away. The torch bearer, who happened to be wheelchair bound, became an instantaneous hero in China for not letting the torch be taken away. Chinese nationals became indignant over the slight to their national pride. In protest, the Chinese public boycotted Carrefour, one of the earliest and most popular hypermarket chains in China, and one of the most well-known French brands in China. Calls to boycott goods from Carrefour spread quickly through social media. However, while Carrefour's sales were hurt in the immediate aftermath of the Olympic torch incident, by 2012 the retail giant posted a 10.8 percent growth, and stated plans to add 20 new outlets each year (Li 2013). While these consumer-led protests elicit much attention in the short term, it is unclear if they actually lead to any long-term effects.

Not everyone is comfortable with the conflation of patriotism and consumerism, however. Some, especially those in first-tier cities who had more everyday access to foreign cultures, took a more restrained view. Zhu Long, the Apple products enthusiast we met in the chapter on Spaces, made a connection between Japanese and Chinese production.

I don't think boycotting Japanese goods is a good idea. Actually what happens is that we Chinese will lose in the end. Many investors in the Japanese companies are Chinese or people from other countries. And the related upstream and downstream enterprises are Chinese. By boycotting Japanese goods, we harm the development of the Chinese enterprises. It is not wise.

Yin Feng, the online gamer, took the issue another step further, arguing that boycotts hurt the fundamental right that citizens have to consume freely.

My opinion is that we should not do to others what we would not have them do to us. We consumers have the right to choose among brands, but we should not impose our decisions on other people. Let's not let this so-called patriotic mood become an excuse for hatred. Once the patriotic mood becomes blinded by craziness, it also becomes a tool to hurt other people. Under the trend of global integration, it is impossible for China to exist independently by getting rid of the world. China has not only introduced a large amount of imported goods, but also exports goods overseas. This exchange has increased people's living standards. We should not boycott blindly because, in the end, we give up our own freedom.

Like the boycott of foreign goods, the 2008 Beijing Olympics can also evoke mixed reactions. When I spoke with people just on the eve of the Olympics, the nearly unanimous reaction was pride in what they felt was China's emergence onto the global stage as a bona fide world power. The event evoked the deepest feelings of national pride. However, four years later and upon deeper reflection, people were less uniformly positive. They mentioned the financial cost of the event, which did nothing to help China's poor. Some pointed to the fact that massive and expensive constructions, like the Bird's Nest Stadium, stood largely empty yet required high maintenance costs. Yin Feng said bitterly that the government should have done more for the victims of the Chengdu earthquake, which also occurred in 2008, and killed an estimated 68,000 people.

I didn't have time to pay attention to the Olympics, it was just an exercise in our leaders' vanity. The earthquake was much more important. I couldn't eat because of all of the devastation. I wish more people could have cared about that.

THE ENVIRONMENT

In February 2013, a Chinese entrepreneur by the name of Jin Zengmin became tired of officials claiming the water in a nearby river, which had become black and oily from industrial runoff, posed no environmental hazards. This river in Zhejiang province was, according to Jin, where villagers used to wash vegetables and clothes when he was a child. He posted photos on *Weibo*, claiming the environmental bureau was turning a blind eye. In a move widely shared in social media, he offered his local environmental protection bureau chief 200,000 yuan ($32,000) to swim in the river. The officer declined, but offered no solution for cleaning up the pollution.

Just a month later, Zhejiang became the scene of another environmental catastrophe. Sixteen thousand dead pigs were found in the tributaries of the Huangpu river, a source of tap water that served residents of nearby Shanghai. Tests showed that the pigs carried porcine circovirus, a disease common among hogs but not known to be infectious to humans. While farmers are required by law to send animals that have the disease to processing pits, black-market dealers intercept the chain, butchering the hogs to sell as pork. Because of harsher crackdowns on this illegal trade, black-market traders had stopped buying the infected pigs, and farmers resorted to dumping them in the river. Meanwhile, Shanghai's municipal water department continued to maintain that the water from the river was safe to drink. While discussions have sprouted up throughout the country's microblogging networks, organized protests have been quickly shut down (Davison 2013).

Not long after this, 1,000 duck carcasses were found floating in Sichuan province's Nanhe river. The rotten birds had been found tucked into fifty woven plastic bags. While the river is not a source of drinking water and thus, according to authorities, poses no threat to public health, the public nonetheless demanded answers. People have been most vocal on microblogging sites. One poster, with the user name of Baby Lucky, posted "Dead pigs, dead ducks . . . this soup is getting thicker and thicker." Despite the silence on the part of Chinese authorities, by one estimate, 40 percent of China's rivers have been classified as "seriously polluted" (Grenoble 2013).

China's air quality has also come under intense scrutiny. Leading up to the 2008 Olympics, air pollution levels were reported to be two to three times higher than levels deemed safe by the World Health Organization. Athletes arrived as late as possible to limit exposure, setting up in neighboring Japan and South Korea to train right up to the event. During a visit in early 2013, I found Beijing cloaked in a haze that was so thick, the portrait of Mao Zedong above the gate to the Forbidden City was nearly obscured. The problem is a combination of continued reliance on coal, factory pollutants from oil and power companies, and the ever-increasing number of automobiles clogging China's cities. Analyses of China's economic policies point to even greater surges in coal consumption and automobile sales over the next decade. For example, the number of passenger cars in China is on track to hit 400 million by 2030 (Wong 2013). The air pollution is said to kill nearly 700,000 people a year (Stout 2013).

As with water pollution, air quality has become a huge topic in the online world, with microbloggers exerting enormous pressure on government officials to take action. As a result, more than eighty cities have begun to monitor and publish real-time data on air pollutants. Environmentalist Ma Jun and his team at the non-profit Institute of Public and Environmental Affairs (IPE) have launched a social media mapping program, dubbed "take a picture to locate a polluter," that exposes China's biggest polluters. Ma and others like him have become social media watchdogs, keeping the public as informed as possible under a state system that, for over half a century, has sought to control the news (Stout 2013).

China's highest ranking officials have taken note of the public's anger, with a growing number openly acknowledging the problem. In his inaugural speech, President Li Keqiang spoke candidly about being "depressed" by the pollution shrouding the capital city, and encouraged the media and the public to hold him accountable for cleaning up polluted water and food supplies. "Poverty and backwardness in the midst of clear waters and verdant mountains is no good," he said, "nor is it to have prosperity and wealth while the environment deteriorates" (Jacobs 2013).

I have personally observed a dramatic change in people's attitudes towards the environment. Just a decade ago, nobody mentioned environmental degradation as a concern. Today, by contrast, a growing number of people spontaneously bring up the negative consequences of consumption, directly connecting their own consumer behaviors with changes in their environment. While not all consumers are activists or try to spread information to the public, there is a growing sense of urgency about the state of China's natural world. In addition, there is a growing awareness that this is not just a macro-problem, but one that can be addressed at the personal level. Ji Ying Jiang, the father of a newborn we met in the chapter on Commodification, had this to say: "All the people should protect the environment. For example, people like to throw garbage everywhere and there is a lot of it near tourist attractions."

He went on to link pollution to the insatiable appetite for consumption.

Sometimes, the action of purchasing something is impulsive. Many people just buy because they say, "I like it," but the products don't meet real needs that they have. So they end up with too many electronic products, clothes or bags that are very similar. Likewise, they buy disposable dishware for convenience. But this ends up leading to huge amounts of waste.

Yi Fei Tian, a 50-year-old male college administrator, put it in patriotic terms:

> Personally, we can do some simple and small things for the environment. For example, turn off the light when we leave the room, take public transportation when going out, use energy-saving lamps, sort garbage, and reuse resources. These are just small things that we can do easily but they are really good for our environment. It is not only the government's duty, but everyone's duty to build our homeland.

CONSUMER RIGHTS

Food safety is another area in which consumers in China are increasingly demanding accountability and transparency. In 2008, over 300,000 babies fell ill after being fed Chinese-made formula that had been adulterated with melamine. The melamine was added to boost the protein content of the formula. At least six infants died from consuming this baby milk. The scandal caused immense outrage about the lack of food-safety standards among domestic companies, which do not have the same strict requirements that global corporations impose. Anxious parents purchased international brands over domestic ones, even buying out all of the baby formula in Hong Kong, where food safety standards are thought to be much higher.

The baby formula scandal was only one of several cases that became widely talked about by the general public. Just a few years earlier, a domestic brand of soy sauce was found to be made of hair clippings. Ink and paraffin were found in instant noodles. Pork buns were discovered to be so loaded with bacteria that they glowed in the dark. Formaldehyde has been found in cabbage, and chlorine in soft drinks (McDonald 2012). On my most recent trip to China in May 2013, officials arrested 904 suspects for passing off bogus beef, which was in fact made out of fox, mink, and rat.

Food contamination stories show up almost daily in social media. Nascent but quickly growing forms of consumer activism are spreading, especially online. The China Survival Guide iPhone app was downloaded 200,000 times within the first week of its launch. It gives out daily updates on issues, organizing them into the categories of health, nutrition, dairy, and beverages. Wu Heng's "Throw it out the window" is a food scandal database that alerts the public to the dangers at the supermarket and in restaurants. His 30 volunteers help him post information on food safety scandals around the country, which are also broadcast over *Weibo*.

Surprisingly, state officials have publicly backed Wu Heng and his site, with the Shanghai food safety officials actually linking his site to their website. This is seen as a positive indication of the state's willingness to allow consumers the right to exchange information about companies. Some see this as a positive first step towards the establishment of formalized consumer protection structures; others are not so sure the state will allow true consumer freedom of speech. In fact, Beijing writer, Zhao Lianhai, was sentenced to two and a half years in jail for "inciting social disorder" after he organized parents of children sickened by tainted milk in 2008.

Consumers thus feel that they need to take matters into their own hands as much as possible. In addition to monitoring news on social media, they purchase more expensive international brands over domestic ones, when the choice is there. Western-style hypermarkets, such as Carrefour and WalMart, are also thought to be backed by stricter standards than small Chinese stores. As we explored in a previous chapter, part of the reason for the immense success of Western fast-food restaurants such as McDonald's is in their reputation for having high standards of hygiene. Choosing international brands over domestic ones is one key strategy Chinese consumers have to feel more in control of the safety of their food.

CENSORSHIP

When I first lived in China, it was 1990, just one year after the Tiananmen Square democracy demonstrations that eventually ended in the crackdown of June 4, 1989. These events shocked the world because, up until then, we had all assumed that democracy would develop alongside capitalism in China. The reforms instituted under Deng Xiaoping starting in 1978 did not include political freedom, however. The government remains a one-party, authoritarian regime. Despite the increased "freedom" to consume, other civic freedoms have not followed. Governmental leaders are not chosen by popular vote, but by a secretive process among the political elite. Furthermore, citizen rights have developed unevenly and are often subject to unexpected crackdowns. The decision to expand consumer choice but not political choice created dynamics that are fundamental to understanding the Chinese experience (Garon and Maclachlan, 2006).

Whether a true civil society will develop in China alongside economic reforms has been a central question for China watchers. The Tiananmen massacre of 1989, media blackout of riots in Tibet and the Muslim region of Xinjiang, outlawing of the Falun Gong as heretical, numerous high profile cases of dissidents being tried or imprisoned without due legal process, and general secrecy around changes in political power have served to convince China observers that the answer is not yet. By most scholarly accounts, China has not yet developed a true public sphere in the Habermasian sense of an independent space between the private and the state, where citizens can challenge state authority.

In terms of freedom of speech, China has one of the most comprehensive systems of media censorship in the world. Traditional media, including newspapers, radio, and television, are owned by the CCP. Consequently, key posts in these organizations are held by party leaders, ensuring fairly rigid compliance when it comes to what is aired and what is not. The CCP also runs a Central Propaganda Department, which directs all of the media outlets in terms of what to air. Topics that have been censored include anything about the Tiananmen Square protests of 1989, Falun Gong, Tibet, police brutality, religious content, and democracy movements (Minemura 2010). Negative accounts of the CCP and materials from other countries that conflict with official Chinese versions of historical events are also censored. The media outlets that are censored include television, print, film, theater, literature, and the internet. China's level of censorship was ranked "very serious" in 2013 by *Reporters Without Borders*.

The online world is also limited in the sense that authorities restrict access to certain websites and to certain keyword searches. Banned sites include YouTube, Facebook, Twitter, and Wikipedia – all sites that have been associated with democracy movements elsewhere in the world. Although Google is available in China, it is a Chinese version of Google that restricts searches on sensitive topics. Access to certain bloggers with anti-CCP views are also blocked, as well as some international news sites such as the BBC. While censorship is vast, authorities also count on a certain measure of self-censorship among internet users. Through certain high profile arrests, the state has created a climate of fear and insecurity in the internet population, who can never be entirely sure of how much their daily activities are actually being monitored. Another tactic the state uses is employing "web commentators" who regularly direct internet discussions on forums and social media into pro-CCP views. All of these methods are cheekily known as China's "Great Firewall," a play on the Great Wall, which was meant to keep out foreign intruders (Herold and Marolt 2011).

These restrictions, however do not mean that Chinese users have absolutely no access to certain content and sites. Rather, savvy Chinese internet users have created ways of bypassing censorship and control through using proxy servers. They also talk about topics indirectly, using substitute phrases that are made up of different characters, yet which sound similar to the words they have in mind. This use of phonograms allows microblogs to escape the automatic red flagging that happens when certain words are used. The foreigner even with an advanced grasp of Chinese characters can still find these microblog posts confusing, as they make use of very clever and subtle substitutions. As Marolt argues:

> Just as the regime is deploying highly flexible, multi-pronged, and increasingly subtle forms of control and censorship to prevent the spread of undesirable content, so are Chinese netizens creating ever more imaginative ways in which individual internet users bypass (rather than engage) the hegemonic narratives of censorship and control. (2011: 57)

Michael Anti (aka Jing Zhao) is a key figure in China's new journalism, and has been blogging from behind the Great Firewall for twelve years. In a TED Talk on the topic of the internet, he points out that Chinese microbloggers are quite different than Twitter users elsewhere in the world. Because of the nature of the written language, 140 characters can express much more than 140 letters in English. Microblogs thus often reflect complete thoughts, as opposed to just headlines. He argues that social media such as *Weibo* microblogging represent a new and growing kind of public sphere in China, where strangers negotiate with each other to express their ideas. *Weibo* is not just another media, is has become *the* media, with over 300 million users in China. He argues that "As far as the Chinese are concerned, if something is not on *Weibo*, it does not exist" (Anti 2012).

Wen Long, a 23-year-old male who lives in Mianyang and is an active microblogger, put it this way:

> We live both in the real world and virtual worlds. In the virtual world, people can use technology to do something different from the real world. We can live different lifestyles in this world. It is immediate. The internet gives us the opportunity to realize complete freedom.

In terms of television, CNN is allowed only in some places such as multi-national hotels. However, the signal is delayed by ten seconds, allowing authorities to black out any politically sensitive segments before they air. In 2013, luxury product advertisements were banned from TV as well as radio, in an attempt to appease a public weary of the political elite's spending habits. Television content focused on fantasy, time travel, and other mythical stories have also been banned. In an attempt to control the influence of foreign cultures, foreign TV shows can no longer air during prime time. Even the extremely popular reality singing show *Super Girl*, a copycat of *American Idol*, was banned for being morally superficial.

In film, not every Hollywood blockbuster will make it through China's censors. Films with sexually explicit content, such as *Brokeback Mountain* and *Memoirs of a Geisha*, were not shown in cinemas. The globally successful third *Pirates of the Caribbean* movie was banned because the ten minutes of footage containing actor Chow Yun-fat was deemed a negative portrayal of the Chinese people. Bans on films, however, have little effect in terms of what the public has access to. Pirated DVDs, downloads via peer-to-peer networks online, and international friends who bring copies of movies all prove the porousness of the Great Firewall in a time of increased global contact, both online and offline.

Likewise, books officially banned in China still make their way into readers' hands. Taiwan and Hong Kong, popular destinations for travelers, each enjoy the right of a free press. It is not uncommon to find mainlanders carrying back stacks of books, as the only penalty for being caught is having the book confiscated. With so many travelers crossing the border between Hong Kong and the mainland, the majority of book smugglers cross over with their banned items successfully. Furthermore, the growing audience for electronic books makes sharing even easier across borders and within networks.

THEORETICAL CONSIDERATIONS

Consumers in China are not uniformly positive about consumer culture. As we explored in this chapter, deep ambivalences surface as they consider whether excessive consumption threatens morality, personal safety, and the environment. From consumers' own point of view, consumption is in turns liberating and problematic, cosmopolitan and a threat to Chinese tradition. This chapter has explored some of the growing ways in which people express their awareness of the negative consequences of consumption, and how nascent but growing forms of activism among the Chinese public are starting to disrupt both state control and corporate misdemeanors. It has become increasingly problematic for the state to control free speech while allowing its citizens to consume freely. As we have seen, individuals are drawing upon their identities as consumers to demand certain rights and protections. From the tainted milk scandal to the reactions to Japan over disputed islands, Chinese nationals are turning to their roles as consumers to create opportunities for change in ways that were not possible before the internet.

From a theoretical perspective, one key question that emerges is whether or not China is developing a true public sphere. Jürgen Habermas' concept of the public sphere remains the most influential foundational framework in terms of understanding how ideas are exchanged among citizens outside private, domestic life (1989). He describes the public sphere as the space that arises whenever two or more people come together to talk about matters of common concern. In such a sphere, people come together to articulate, distribute, and negotiate meanings. In Habermas' historical analysis of eighteenth-century Europe, he notes that growing rates of literacy, accessibility to literature, and the burgeoning of critical journalism, all contributed to a lively public domain that remained free from state and church authorities. Habermas' conception of the public sphere centered on locations such as coffee houses and salons – areas of society where people of all walks of life could (at least in theory) gather and discuss matters that concerned them.

Much has been written about the possibilities for a democratic space to arise in China, either state sanctioned or in defiance of the state. Likewise, recent work on the internet in China has focused on its potential role as a kind of virtual public sphere, where users can voice their concerns in communal settings. While the literature on China's democratic process is vast, the general consensus is that the citizens have not yet been able to develop a "true" public sphere, in the original Habermasian sense. As we have observed in this chapter, the Chinese state does not guarantee freedom of speech, continuing to monitor public arenas for anything regarded as subversive or anti-government. While social media forms such as *Weibo* and QQ have contributed to a burgeoning of public self-expression, at the same time, self-censorship practices have emerged in efforts to evade state monitoring.

I would argue that in understanding consumption in China today, we need to shift the focus away from framing the dynamics strictly in terms of a Western-derived conception of the public sphere. China may not be following an evolutionary model that ends with the development of a public sphere like that of the USA and Western European democratic countries. What we see emerging in China is a model of overlapping rather than distinct spheres of influence. If we visualize these spheres as overlapping circles, one circle represents the sphere of consumption, the second the sphere of capitalism, and the third the sphere of the state. In the overlapping spheres, particular forms of expression and even activism arise. When it comes to concern around the environment, food safety, or combating corruption, some forms of activism actually support state goals, while others become coopted by the state. The consumer boycotts of Japanese products, for example, supported and mirrored the Chinese state's reactions to Japan's claim on a contested group of islands.

There are also parts of each circle that do not overlap with any of the others. In recent years, consumers have begun publicly to expose producers who sell contaminated or counterfeit products, particularly those that put people's health at risk. The state has largely stayed out of this debate, allowing the consumer public sphere to grow in terms of this conversation. But the experience of an "independent" consumer space of expression is not necessarily in a state of continuous growth. Rather, what we observe in China is its expansion and contraction in relation to larger socio-political events.

Nonetheless, in considering that space of consumption which operates independently of the state and producers, what we see is an emerging *consumer public sphere*. It is similar to the Habermasian public sphere in that it represents a space (whether in the physical or virtual world) where people come together to discuss matters freely. However, it differs from the original concept in that it is, at its foundation, a sphere of consumption (Zukin 2004). When people enter into this "space," they do so primarily as consumers, with consumer issues in mind. In the absence of a true political democracy in China, consumerism has become an alternative pathway to structural change, as microbloggers expose corrupt corporate practices, and everyday citizens boycott goods from certain nations. While we should not conflate consumerism with the wider notion of a public sphere, the emerging consumer public sphere has become an influential "third space" that, at times, can operate independently of both state and corporate interests. It is not the coffee houses and salons of Habermas' original study where such a sphere is being formed, but rather, the consumer spaces in both the physical and virtual worlds.

7 Consumption with Chinese Characteristics

This book has explored consumer culture in China from various vantage points, each one highlighting different sets of dynamics at play. Throughout the chapters, I have sought to frame what is happening in China within the context of the enormous changes that have occurred over the last few decades. The consumer oriented culture that we can observe in China – or more precisely, in China's urban centers – is the outcome of very rapid transformations in the economy and social structures. I often observe business people new to China take consumer culture in China as a given, viewing the enormous opportunities in a historical vacuum. When we view the state of the present within a broader historical context, we can better understand why consumer culture has developed the way it has in China. In this final chapter, we will return to the question posed in the introductory chapter: In what ways does China's consumer revolution follow universal patterns, and in what ways is it unique?

As we have seen throughout the chapters, in many ways, China's consumer culture mirrors what has been documented among the more mature consumer cultures. Just as Karl Marx observed in Western Europe, daily life in China under capitalism has become increasingly commodified and subject to market values. As Thorstein Veblen observed in turn-of-the-century USA, conspicuous consumption has come to define the expression of status in China, as the upwardly mobile surround themselves with luxury brands and other "must haves." French sociologist Michel Maffesoli described the move from traditional tribes, based on static and unified notions of geographic and kinship, to neo-tribes, which can come into being as occasions arise. As we've seen in China, consumers are forming online as well as offline communities based on their consumer affiliations as well as their desires for activism. Michel de Certeau argued against the idea that consumers were passive victims of corporate brainwashing, and posited that their everyday "tactics of consumption" can lead to self-realized, resistant, and creative selves. Likewise, what we see in China is a growing sense of agency connected to consumption, as consumers reinvent and reimagine themselves through their consumer choices. As Daniel Miller observed in London malls, shopping, place, and identity are closely intertwined concepts. In China, virtual and real spaces of consumption have become important staging areas for the expression of sociality and subjectivity. These are certainly not the only areas in which the experiences of China's consumers parallel those of the more modern capitalistic economies, but they represent some of the most salient validations of global consumption theory.

However, other experiences among China's consumers do not fit neatly into prevailing frameworks. This concluding chapter explores the dynamics that differentiate Chinese consumer experiences from dominant models of consumption, based primarily on Western societies. The five main themes that have emerged include virtu-real experiences, status experimentations, brand ideologies, multiple nodes of cosmopolitanism, and the contested sphere of the consumer public.

VIRTU-REAL EXPERIENCES

When it comes to sites of consumption, the literature largely focuses on physical realms – shopping malls, supermarkets, and entertainment destinations. Analyses of online activities are growing, but still tend to be treated as secondary and separate from the "primary" realms of shopping in the "real" world. Furthermore, online activity in China tends to be analyzed through the lens of public sphere, political activity, and freedom of expression. The general consensus of such studies is that while the internet has opened up opportunities for Chinese citizens to self-organize, it is still a limited realm because of censorship, and thus not yet a "true" public sphere. China's internet, thus, is seen as fundamentally constrained through this Western lens. Such an approach obscures the reality that the online world is incredibly diverse, dynamic, and innovative in terms of how people are communicating, sharing, and consuming. Online commerce, and all the related social media sharing that goes along with it, should be viewed as what it is: an immensely pleasurable and complex space of expression and sociality.

Furthermore, the internet should not be viewed as fundamentally separate from other consumption activities, or somehow secondary to the activities in the real world of shopping and commerce. In China, consumers move fluidly between online and offline spaces when they consume. They use their smartphones to access the mobile internet, and move back and forth between social media and physical spaces to discuss, plan, experience, and share their consumption activities. For younger Chinese in particular, consumer activities are incomplete without the component of online social sharing. Such fluidity between virtual and real contexts are only increasing as more people acquire smartphones and are able to experience enhanced consumer activities that transcend specific geographic locations.

In this, China is not unique, as the mobile internet becomes accessible to more people around the world, but particularly in emerging markets, where smartphone ownership even outpaces computer ownership. Smartphones are the cheapest entry into the online world. They foster "always on" forms of communication and consumption, as acts in the "real world" become conversational pieces in the virtual world, and decisions in the virtual world become enacted in the real world. Despite the fact that China is decades behind the developed world when it comes to capitalistic practices, it leads the world when it comes to virtu-real consumer practices. The ecosystem of online resources in China connected to commerce – ranging from social media to review sites to photo sharing sites to mobile wallet apps – creates consumption processes that interconnect physical and virtual realms in an increasingly seamless way. What we see among China's hip, urban, socially connected, and technologically savvy consumers is potentially what we may see in other countries as their populations begin to adopt mobile internet devices. In this sense, China's consumer culture may be analyzed as a potential predictor of what could happen elsewhere.

As such, it is important within consumption theory to acknowledge the transcendent nature of "spaces" and create frameworks that reflect the emerging practices we see in China as well as elsewhere among mobile internet users. As we have seen in the case of consumers in China, social status, conspicuous consumption, neo-tribe affiliations, and consumer activism span virtual and physical contexts. In addition, as we have seen in an increasing number of cases in China, the so-called "real" contexts of the physical world become secondary sites of consumption, as the virtual world takes precedence – particularly in the area of consumer activism. Geographer Doreen Massey offers a direction to follow for a more fluid way of conceptualizing space, which allows for the inclusion of multiple forms. As she puts it, space is not just the flat land upon which we walk, but also a dimension of multiplicity. Space, in this more conceptual form, is made up of our relations and connections with each other, which are, of course, fraught with inequality and power differentials (2005). Following Massey's suggestion, we can frame the intersections between the virtual and the physical as a social space, within which consumer connections are expressed, fostered, harnessed, and exploited. As consumers develop new paths through these emerging spaces, they create different forms of social dynamics and desire fulfillment.

STATUS EXPERIMENTATIONS

The convergence of an unprecedented scale of economic development and China's first Singleton generation has produced a generation that does not have established norms around status to emulate. They cannot look to their parents and grandparents as models, for the latter grew up under a system which sought to eradicate class differences. They also cannot look to an entrenched elite, as the CCP effectively dismantled the upper class of pre-Mao China. While party members and affiliates represent a kind of elite, they are not looked upon as models for status building in post-reform China. Rather, the political elite and their offspring are typically typecast as having outrageous and offensive spending habits – and the feelings are especially negative coming from the younger generation.

Nonetheless, social distinctions are making a strong comeback in China, after several decades during which Mao Zedong dismantled the class system and effectively abolished social difference based on wealth and status. However, as we have seen, conventional ways of defining status through class do not adequately reflect the social forms that are emerging in China. This is due to many factors. It is objectively difficult to define class boundaries in China because of the vast discrepancies in wealth between rural and urban and between different urban centers. Median incomes, thus, do not reflect the realities of the variation in lifestyles. Data on how much people make can also be misleading due to factors such as the practice of New Year's bonuses, which go unreported. Furthermore, households in China have very different make-ups than those in other developed markets, as young adults with professional incomes tend to live with their parents until they get married. The One-Child Policy and the "4-2-1 phenomenon" of parents and grandparents doting on their one descendant have also resulted in a young adult population with higher spending capacity than their peers elsewhere in the world. Global measures of class distinctions based on objective factors such as household income are thus difficult to apply to China.

More importantly, what we see is that consumers in China do not think in class terms. They hold varied and inconsistent definitions of what it means to be middle or upper class. But more importantly, consumers in China prefer to describe themselves as not yet having reached a particular class status. This is not so much a sense of modesty or false modesty, but rather, a strong belief that class is too static a concept to reflect their own lifestyles. Rather than place themselves in a class category, they prefer to think of themselves as upwardly mobile, and in a state of change rather than a defined state. Related to this, what we see in China is the desire to link status with entrepreneurialism, hard work, and one's own initiative. In this sense, we can add an additional form of conspicuousness to Thorsten Veblen's original framework. "Conspicuous accomplishment" more adequately reflects the dynamics of status in China, as people seek to demonstrate their *nengli*, or personal capabilities and entrepreneurialism, in their consumption choices.

As the self-described upwardly mobile seek to defy the constrictions of bounded categories such as class, we also see the younger generation co-opting class terms and reformulating them to reflect emerging lifestyles. *Xiaozi*, which originally referred to the petite bourgeoisie, has come to stand for China's new culture of self-indulgence. Here, we see a complete reversal of Mao's socialist ideology of self-sacrifice for the nation, rejection of Western/colonial influences, and de-prioritization of leisure activities. Instead, the self-described *xiaozi* seek out opportunities for lifestyles based around prioritizing pleasure and desire fulfillment. Young Chinese have taken a concept that was originally based on the idea of production, as the petite bourgeoisie were defined as the owners of small businesses, and made it into a celebratory lifestyle statement.

Much of the literature on China's consumer culture, particularly emerging from the business sphere, takes class for granted. Middle-class identity, in particular, is typically conflated with middle-income levels, and as such, middle classness is framed as an inevitable outcome of economic growth. Drawing inspiration from Mark Liechty, who investigated the intersections of consumerism, youth culture, media, and class in Nepal in the mid-1990s, I would suggest that instead of treating any form of status as a natural, universal category, we instead attempt to explain it through everyday consumer experiences. Status is intertwined with cultural life and the result of cultural strategies. As Liechty argues, "The middle class is a constantly renegotiated cultural space – a space of ideas, values, goods, practices, and embodied behaviors – in which the terms of inclusion and exclusion are endlessly tested, negotiated, and affirmed. From this point of view, it is the process, not the product, that constitutes class" (2003: 15).

Likewise, I would also argue that instead of assuming the existence of a middle class in China, we investigate consumers' actual strategies of inclusion and exclusion – as Liechty puts. What we see is a desire by Chinese consumers themselves to frame status differently in terms of one's potential and work ethic, as opposed to purely one's income and related lifestyle. What consumers in China seek is to convey their aspirational narratives and their capacity for self-created change. Any language we use to frame social distinctions needs to account for such motivations, whether we rethink what class means in a China context, or create new ways of talking about social status that better reflect consumers' everyday behaviors.

BRAND IDEOLOGIES

In the dichotomy of structure versus agency, it is tempting to view consumerism in China in the framework of increased individual agency.

In this narrative, the Chinese state is retreating from its heavy-handed structuring of people's everyday lives, which prevailed during the decades of Mao Zedong's rule. Marketers and business people, in particular, are very much enamored with the idea that consumption in China has led to more individual freedom to choose one's own, authentic lifestyle. From the academic perspective, the postmodern consumption literature also focuses heavily on how consumers forge and experiment with new identities through their consumption behaviors. Such scholars emphasize the pleasure, enjoyment, and escape of consumption, challenging earlier frameworks that focused on structure and social hierarchy. Consumption was thus viewed as liberatory and a space for democratic expression (see Fiske 2000).

The reality that I have observed over the last few decades, however, is not quite as celebratory. While the state has retreated in some aspects of people's daily lives, it has been replaced by a new kind of structuring power, represented by product and service brands. As we have seen throughout this book, brands play an enormous role in everyday lives. When people, and especially young people, talk about their social affiliations, their aspirations, and their own identities, they more often than not refer to brands. They refer to themselves in relation to these brands – what it means to be a Jeep owner, an iPhone user, or a Gucci wearer. Global corporations continuously feed into the seemingly insatiable desire to associate one's self with brands that represent different facets of identity in new, "modernizing" China.

As the state once created structure of status as part of its holistic ideology, corporations now fill that void through the use of brand ideologies. Individuals use brands – and in particular, global luxury or status brands – to signify their values and aspirations. They use brands as entrees into new forms of belonging. Brands have thus become a kind of shortcut way of describing one's self (see Lukacs 2010). Chinese consumers are not unique in the world in terms of their desire to associate themselves with brands. But what is unique is the velocity with which brands have come to structure Chinese consumer identities.

The incredible desire for branded products has led to some controversial behaviors, which have become topics of national conversation through social media. The teenager who sold a kidney to buy an iPhone, the couple who sold an infant daughter to buy luxury clothing, the young woman who declared she would rather be unhappy in the back of a BMW than in love on the back of a bike — these well-publicized examples underscore the new kind of structuring force that brands play in everyday consumer lives. They represent desired lifestyles.

Nonetheless, there are indications that Marx does not get the last word in here, and that consumers in China are not uniformly victimized by capitalists. In some cases, they are actively reinventing these brands, and in turn, corporations are adapting to mirror back what their customers seek from them. We see this in the way consumers in China have inverted some of the meanings around Western fast-food brands, which carry very different associations in China. These brands have responded by recasting their own identities in China, offering different products, and most importantly, continually inviting consumers in China to participate actively in these brand experiences. In this sense, brand identities can be viewed as the outcomes of conversations between producers and consumers, rather than simply the imposition of one's strategies upon the other.

Brands represent the new ideologies that structure daily lives in China. Gone are the Communist propaganda posters, exhorting people to strive towards a socialist utopia. They are replaced by advertisements that connect beauty, success, and love not only to consumption, but to specific brands. Whether consumers are walking around with knock-offs or saving up for a trip to Paris to shop at the real Gucci store, they are desiring not only the objects, but the lifestyles that these objects represent. To understand consumption among the Chinese today, we must view their engagement with products and services as brand experiences, with their own logics and structuring capabilities.

MULTIPLE NODES OF COSMOPOLITANISM

Compared to three decades ago, people in China have vastly more opportunities to connect with the world outside their country. Under Mao Zedong's rule, the country closed itself off to foreign investment and most forms of foreign influence. Travel outside China was extremely restricted. Only in the last two decades have restrictions been lifted, and only in the last decade have ordinary citizens had the means of paying for travel abroad. In addition to physical forms of travel, consumers in China can experience foreign cultures through multiple media forms. Korean K-pop and soap operas, Hong Kong fashion, Japanese manga, American movies, and Western fast food have become a normalized part of urban consumer lifestyles.

Everyday lives in China are increasingly touched by processes of globalization. Globalization can be defined as "the process in which consumers, corporations and government are increasingly interconnected across national borders through the media, capital exchanges, production and consumption" (Hall 2002). Academics do not agree on the outcomes of globalization. On one end of the spectrum are studies that view globalization as a destroyer of the local and authentic. These studies focus on the so-called "McDonaldization" of urban spaces, as the authentic makes way to a mass, global culture originating from the West (Ritzer 2000). On the other end of the spectrum are studies that celebrate globalization and transnational processes, focusing on the "freely" flowing stream of media, information, cultures, people, and money across borders (Appadurai 1990).

The reality for consumers in China spans this spectrum. China's cities are becoming increasingly homogenized, looking more like other cities in developed Asia as older neighborhoods are torn down to build the same kinds of malls and skyscrapers one can find in Singapore, Seoul, and Taipei. On the other hand, globalization has led to increased opportunities for education, career, and self-expression for China's citizens. The desire to become more knowledgeable about the world outside their immediate experience is a strong motivator of consumer behaviors in China. People are looking to travel as a way to make them "modern" in the sense of being more knowledgeable through physical as well as social mobility. In *Desiring China*, Lisa Rofel explores the themes of postsocialist modernity and identity constructions. In it, she offers a conceptual connection between cosmopolitanism and consumption. "Consumption is about embodiment, embodying a new self. At the heart of this embodiment is desire. A properly cosmopolitan self is supposed to be desirous and this desire is supposed to be open and unconstrained" (2007: 118).

What is often misunderstood, however, is the nature of cosmopolitanism in China, which is often interpreted as a desire to become more Western. Instead, Chinese forms of cosmopolitanism incorporate multiple nodes of influence. These include the West for sure, but also integrate the "Global East" as well as transnational China. South Korea, for example, has come to represent a vision of a thoroughly "modern" yet "authentically Asian" consumer culture, which consumers in China seek to emulate. Returnees – Chinese nationals who have studied and worked abroad – are also a source of cultural capital because of their international experience and ability to thrive across borders. Instead of merely emulating the West, Chinese forms of cosmopolitanism are complex, multi-nodal, and characterized by the desire to express both globalism and "Chineseness" at the same time. As Aihwa Ong and Donald Nonini argue, within the global capitalist economy are competing modernities (1997).

Cosmopolitanism in China is also defined by a kind of nostalgia for a vanishing "tradition," often represented through exotic domestic locations. Tibet, Xinjiang, Hainan, and Mongolia represent the far away, child-like, and strange. Rural locations similarly represent the purity and simplicity that are the antithesis of modern urban lifestyles. By desiring the exotic and the rural, urban Chinese define themselves as modern against the distinctly unmodern "others" of China's hinterlands. The desire to consume the pure and traditional is yet another way consumers express their own cosmopolitanism.

Such phenomenon of hybridized, multi-nodal forms of cosmopolitanism is not unique to China. Consumers in South Korea, Japan, Taiwan, and Singapore are similarly staking out new forms of modernity that integrate as well as go beyond the Western model. The experiences of consumers in China, as well as throughout modern and modernizing Asia, throw into question the common assumption that there is a global consumer culture with the US model as the ultimate endpoint. I would argue that in order to understand properly the effects of globalization on China and emerging forms of cosmopolitanism, we need to disentangle multiple cultural influences and forms of knowledge. What casual observers of China may take as Westernization is in fact a complex mix of Global East, Global West, and uniquely Chinese sensibilities, stewing together to create emerging forms of desire.

THE CONTESTED SPHERE OF THE CONSUMER PUBLIC

What, if any, is the connection between increased freedom to consume and increased freedom in other aspects of daily life in China? The study of consumption can reveal not only how material lives are changing, but also how consumer behaviors bleed over into people's roles as citizens, nationals, or activists. Analysis of agency and empowerment in China typically examine whether a true public sphere has emerged. Jürgen Habermas defined the public sphere as "private people coming together as a public to debate the general rules governing relations in the basically privatized but publicly relevant sphere of commodity exchange and social labor" (1989: 27). Scholars have, over the last few decades since reforms were instituted in China, explored the question of whether a true public sphere would emerge. Most agree that it has not, at least not broadly and not consistently. The internet has played a huge role in creating a free space of dissent and discussion, but as we explored in this book, it is also fraught with restrictions and censorship.

Yet, as Sharon Zukin argues, it is important to consider consumption on its own terms, as a space of significance with regard to empowerment and control, and not merely a trivialized space of shopping. "The revolutionary achievement of mass consumption has been to construct another space between the self and civil society – and by shopping, we place ourselves in this space. Neither completely free nor completely democratic, the public sphere of shopping is a space of discussion and debate. It is a space of manipulation and control, but also of discretion and fulfillment. It is, in fact, an ambiguous or a heterotopic space, where we struggle to combine principles of equality and hierarchy, and pleasure and rationality, to create an experience we value" (2004: 32). Following Zukin, I would argue that in China, the wide space that consumption occupies in daily life has become a new sphere that intersects with both the private and public spheres. As such, it is complex. At times, consumption in China is deeply personal. At other times, as in the case of the boycott of Japanese goods, it can be intensely political.

The role of the state is also complex in our consideration of how truly liberatory the space of consumption is in China. In the power relationship between consumers and producers, the literature wavers between the two. Marx and his followers clearly felt that consumers were the victims in this relationship. Postmodern studies, seeking to counter the image of the consumer as powerless, sought to show how consumption leads to free, self-realized subjectivities. In

China, the reality spans the spectrum. The economy has grown and consumption has expanded enormously not in spite of the Communist state, but *because of* the CCP's concerted efforts to grow the economy and its consumer base. The Chinese Communist Party has not been laissez faire in any sense – through carefully crafted and controlled policies, it has created a vibrant, consuming population. Thus, while consumer culture appears to be ruled by pure market forces, it is in fact closely regulated by the state. For example, as we have seen in our exploration of China's internet, state-driven policies have set the stage for domestic internet companies, such as QQ and Sina, to flourish.

Yet even within this context of a strong state that seeks to control consumer behavior and corporations that seek to entice shoppers to buy more, consumers themselves are nonetheless asserting their agency. In online forums, consumers challenge corporate greed, demand compensation for products that do not fulfill their promises, and expose companies selling counterfeit products. They in fact demand more information about their producers, defying the logic of commodity fetishism. Within the public space of consumption, consumer identities are created and expressed, frustrations vented, and netizens discuss what is moral and ethically correct. People may not be entirely "free" within the space of consumption, but they have used their consumer identities to push for more rights vis-à-vis states and corporations that seek to assert their dominance. As Marolt argues:

> Chinese internet users can't be adequately framed with the European concepts of the civil society or public sphere. The Chinese internet is a highly complex public space inhabited by myriad individuals and groups, permeated with subspaces – particular places of playful and serious consent and dissent, with thoughts and ideas that are continuously produced, remixed, and reproduced across space and time. (2011: 60)

CONSUMPTION WITH CHINESE CHARACTERISTICS

Are consumer revolutions essentially alike or converging towards the endpoint of the dominant model, based primarily on the US and Western European experience? Or are there fundamental differences in the consumption patterns found in China, and for that matter, other consumer cultures developing in the twenty-first century?

As we have seen in this book, China's consumer revolution has followed many of the same patterns as those that occurred elsewhere in the developed world. From commodification to conspicuous forms of consumption, China's consumer patterns validate several enduring consumption theories. At the same time, an exploration of the various facets of consumption in China reveals contextual differences that challenge us to extend consumption theories in light of the changes in technology and global balances of power that have taken place in the last few decades. Following Garon and Maclachlan, I would argue that we cannot assume that the ultimate endpoint is that Chinese consumers will evolve like those in the West (2006). What we see emerging is, to paraphrase Deng Xiaoping, "consumption with Chinese characteristics." When Deng set forth his philosophy of "socialism with Chinese characteristics," what he meant was that China would continue to follow Marxist teaching while domesticating economic practices to suit the state's development goals. It was his sly way of maintaining the appearance of ideological consistency while setting his own course.

Likewise, consumption with Chinese characteristics may appear, on its surface, to follow a kind of global/Western model. The thorough integration of such brands as McDonald's, Starbucks, Disney, and Apple into the everyday lives of people in China seems to confirm this. Yet a deeper look reveals a much more complex, and at times contradictory, consumption landscape. Luxury travel itineraries to Las Vegas, make-up demonstrations for office ladies, Japanese product boycotts, *xiaozi* dreaming of whiling away their time in cafés, mothers exposing their children to cosmopolitan lifestyles through fast-food restaurants, a young woman dreaming of the freedom her Jeep will drive her towards – these stories that make up China's consumer revolution reveal how private and public lives have been transformed in the last thirty years. Consumption in China is much more than just the "triumph" of a Western-style free market. It is the new ideology in China, replacing that of socialism. Like its predecessor, this new ideology has changed the fabric of society, creating new structures, power hierarchies, subjectivities, and futures.

The experiences of consumers in China may help us to uncover consumption frameworks that reflect emerging markets in the Global South and Global East. Countries such as Brazil, Russia, and India are also rapidly developing but with socio-political contexts radically different than the mature consumer markets of the West and Japan. Rather than try to force fit these consumption experiences into our established frameworks, we can approach the development of these new consumer economies as a way of understanding the simultaneously fragmenting and generative nature of consumption. The experiences of consumers in China, living in an immensely transformational period, point us to emerging ways of conceptualizing consumption within the context of new technologies, forms of globalization, and dynamics between states, citizens, and multi-national corporations that seek to penetrate all of people's everyday lives.

References ————————————————————————

Adorno, Theodor W. and Max Horkheimer. 2000. "The culture industry: Enlightenment as mass deception," in Juliet B. Schor and Douglas B. Holt, eds., *The Consumer Society Reader*. New York: The New Press, 3–19.

Anagnost, Ann. 1997. *National Pastimes: Narrative, Representation, and Power in Modern China*. Durham: Duke University Press.

— 2004. "The corporeal politics of quality (suzhi)," *Public Culture*, 16(2).

Anderlini, Jamil. 2010. "Chinese travelers change the face of tourism," *Financial Times*. (online) June 8, 2010. Available at http://www.ft.com/cms/s/0/2b7f47f6-72f0-11df-9161-00144feabdc0.html#axzz2iaUUe21n (accessed October 23, 2013).

Anderson, Benedict. 1983. *Imagined Communities: Reflections on the Origin and Spread of Nationalism*. London: Verso.

Anti, Michael. 2012. "Behind the great firewall of China," *Ted Talks*. (online) June 2012. Available at http://www.ted.com/talks/michael_anti_behind_the_great_firewall_of_china.html (accessed October 23, 2013).

Appadurai, Arjun. 1986. "Introduction: Commodities and the politics of value," in Arjun Appadurai, ed., *The Social Life of Things: Commodities in Cultural Perspective*. Cambridge University Press, 3–63.

— 1990. "Disjuncture and difference in the global cultural economy," in M. Featherstone, ed., *Global Culture*. London: Sage, 295–310.

Arnould, Eric, Linda Price and George Zinkhan, eds. 2004. *Consumers*. New York: McGraw-Hill/Irwin.

Atsmon, Yuvol, Diane Ducarme, Max Magni, and Cathy Wu. 2012. *Luxury Without Borders: China's New Class of Shoppers Take on the World* (online). Available at: http://www.mckinseychina.com/wp-content/uploads/2012/12/the-mckinsey-chinese-luxury-consumer-survey-2012-12.pdf (accessed March 20, 2013).

Baudrillard, Jean. 1998. *The Consumer Society: Myths and Structures*. Thousand Oaks: Sage Publications.

— 2006. *The System of Objects*. New York: Verso.

Benjamin, Walter. 1999. *The Arcades Project*. Cambridge, MA: Harvard University Press.

Boehler, Patrick. 2012. "Chinese tourists to be barred from chic Parisian hotel?" *Time*. (online) October 3, 2012. Available at http://newsfeed.time .com/2012/10/03/chinese-tourists-to-be-barred-from-chic-parisian-hotel/ (accessed October 23, 2013).

Bosker, Bianca. 2013. *Original Copies: Architectural Mimicry in Contemporary China*. Honolulu: University of Hawaii Press.

Bourdieu, Pierre. 1984. *Distinction: A Social Critique of the Judgement of Taste*. London: Routledge & Kegan Paul.

Branigan, Tanya. 2012. "China and cars: A love story," *Guardian*. (online) December 14, 2012. Available at http://www.theguardian.com/world/2012/ dec/14/china-worlds-biggest-new-car-market (accessed October 23, 2013).

Brownell, Susan. 1995. *Training the Body for China: Sports in the Moral Order of the People's Republic*. Chicago: University of Chicago Press.

Business Insider. 2013. "The number of Chinese billionaires passes 300." (online) September 11, 2013. Available at http://www.businessinsider.com/chinese -billionaires-2013-9 (accessed October 24, 2013).

Campanella, Thomas. 2008. *The Concrete Dragon: China's Urban Revolution and What It Means for the World*. Princeton, NJ: Princeton Architecture Press.

Chaney, David. 1996. *Lifestyles*. London: Routledge.

Chen, Xiaoyan and Peng Hwa Ang. 2011. "The Internet police in China: Regulation, scope and myths," in David Kurt Herold and Peter Marolt, eds., *Online Society in China: Creating, Celebrating, and Instrumentalising the Online Carnival*. New York: Routledge, 40–52.

China Internet Network Information Center. "Internet usage in China." (online) Available at http://cpj.org/reports/2013/03/challenged-china-media-censor ship-graphic-internet-use.php (accessed January 20, 2013).

China Luxury Network. Available at http://chinaluxurynetwork.com/ (accessed December 2, 2013).

Chu, Rodney Wai-Chi and Chung-Tai Cheng. 2011. "Cultural convulsions: examining the Chineseness of Cyber China," in David Kurt Herold and Peter Marolt, eds., *Online Society in China: Creating, Celebrating, and Instrumentalising the Online Carnival*. New York: Routledge, 23–39.

Clifford, James. 1992. "Travelling cultures," in Grossberg et al., eds., *Cultural Studies*. New York: Routledge, 96–116.

Cook, Daniel Thomas. 2000. "The rise of 'the toddler' as subject and as merchandising category in the 1930s," in Mark Gottdiener, ed., *New Forms of Consumption*. Boston: Rowman and Littlefield Publishers, Inc, 111–30.

— ed. 2008. *Lived Experiences of Public Consumption: Encounters with Value in Marketplaces on Five Continents.* New York: Palgrave Macmillan.

d'Arpizio, Claudia. 2012. "Chinese shoppers world's top luxury goods spenders," *Bain and Company.* (online) December 12, 2012. Available at http://www.bain.com/about/press/press-releases/bains-china-luxury-market-study-2012.aspx (accessed October 24, 2013).

Davis, Deborah S. 1995. "Introduction: Urban China," in Deborah S. Davis, Richard Kraus, Barry Naughton and Elizabeth J. Perry, eds., *Urban Spaces in China.* New York: Cambridge University Press, 1–19.

— 2000. "Introduction: A revolution in consumption," in Deborah S. Davis, ed., *The Consumer Revolution in Urban China.* Berkeley: University of California Press, 1–22.

— 2005. "Urban consumer culture," *The China Quarterly,* 183: 692–709.

— 2006. "Urban Chinese homeowners as citizen-consumers," in Sheldon Garon and Patricia L. Maclachlan, eds., *The Ambivalent Consumer: Questioning Consumption in East Asia and the West.* Ithaca: Cornell University Press, 281–300.

Davis, Deborah S. and Julia S. Sensenbrenner. 2000. "Commercializing childhood: parental purchases for Shanghai's only child," in Deborah S. Davis, ed., *The Consumer Revolution in Urban China.* Berkeley: University of California Press, 54–79.

Davison, Nicola. 2013. "Rivers of blood: dead pigs rotting in China's water supply," *Guardian.* (online) March 29, 2013. Available at http://www.theguardian.com/world/2013/mar/29/dead-pigs-china-water-supply (accessed October 23, 2013).

De Certeau, Michel. 1984. *The Practice of Everyday Life.* Berkeley: University of California Press.

Doctoroff, Tom. 2005. *Billions: Selling to the New Chinese Consumer.* New York: Palgrave Macmillan.

— 2012. *What Chinese Want: Culture, Communism, and China's Modern Consumer.* New York: Palgrave Macmillan.

Douglas, Mary and Baron Isherwood. 1996. *The World of Goods: Towards an Anthropology of Consumption.* New York: Routledge.

Elsea, Daniel. 2005. "China's chi chi suburbs / American style sprawl all the rage in Beijing," *SFGate.* (online) April 24, 2005. Available at http://www.sfgate.com/opinion/article/China-s-chichi-suburbs-American-style-sprawl-2686119.php (accessed October 23, 2013).

Farrall, Kenneth and David Kurt Herold. 2011. "Identity vs. anonymity: Chinese netizens and questions of identifiability," in David Kurt Herold and Peter

Marolt, eds., *Online Society in China: Creating, Celebrating, and Instrumentalising the Online Carnival*. New York: Routledge, 165–83.

Farrer, James. 2010. "Shanghai bars: Patchwork globalization and flexible cosmopolitanism in reform-era urban-leisure spaces," *Chinese Sociology and Anthropology*, 42(2): 22–38.

Featherstone, Mike. 2007. *Consumer Culture and Postmodernism*. Thousand Oaks: Sage Publications Inc.

Fiske, John. 2000. "Shopping for pleasure: Malls, power, and resistance," in Juliet B. Schor and Douglas B. Holt, eds., *The Consumer Society Reader*. New York: The New Press, 306–28.

Flannery, Russell. 2012. "China mobile phone users now top one billion," *Forbes*. (online) March 30, 2012. Available at http://www.forbes.com/sites/russellflannery/2012/03/30/china-mobile-phone-users-now-exceed-one-billion/ (accessed October 23, 2012).

FlorCruz, Jaime A. 2012. "China's capital still getting kick from 2008 Olympics," *CNN*. (online) July 2, 2012. Available at http://www.cnn.com/2012/07/02/world/asia/china-florcruz-olympics/index.html (accessed October 23, 2013).

Fraser, David. 2000. "Inventing oasis: Luxury housing advertisements and reconfiguring domestic space in Shanghai," in Deborah S. Davis, ed., *The Consumer Revolution in Urban China*. Berkeley: University of California Press, 25–53.

Friedman, Jonathan. 1994. *Cultural Identity and Global Process*. Thousand Oaks: Sage.

Gao, Changxin. 2011. "McDonald's seeking a new menu for mainland success," *China Daily*. (online) August 31, 2011. Available at http://usa.chinadaily.com.cn/epaper/2011-08/31/content_13226801.htm (accessed October 24, 2013).

Garon, Sheldon and Patricia L. Maclachlan. 2006. "Introduction," in Sheldon Garon and Patricia L. Maclachlan, eds., *The Ambivalent Consumer: Questioning Consumption in East Asia and the West*. Ithaca: Cornell University Press, 1–15.

Global Times. 2013. "Africa eyed as vacation spot by more Chinese." (online) Available at http://www.globaltimes.cn/content/771637.shtml#.UmmF9vmTiSo (accessed October 24, 2013).

Godin, Seth. 2008. *Tribes: We Need You To Lead Us*. New York: Penguin Group.

Goffman, Erving. 1959. *The Presentation of Self in Everyday Life*. New York: Anchor.

Gold, Thomas. 1993. "Go with your feelings: Hong Kong and Taiwan Popular Culture in Greater China," *The China Quarterly*, 136, Special Issue: Greater China (Dec. 1993): 907–25.

Goodman, David S. G. 1996. "The People's Republic of China: The party-state, capitalist revolution and new entrepreneurs," in Richard Robison and David S. G. Goodman, eds., *The New Rich in Asia: Mobile Phones, McDonald's and Middle-Class Revolution*. New York: Routledge, 225–42.

— 2008. "Why China has no new middle class: Cadres, managers, and entrepreneurs," in David Goodman, ed., *The New Rich in China: Future Rulers, Present Lives*. New York: Routledge, 23–7.

Gottdiener, M. 2000a. "Approaches to consumption: Classical and contemporary perspectives," in Mark Gottdiener, ed., *New Forms of Consumption: Consumers, Culture, and Commodification*. Lanham: Rowman and Littlefield Publishers, Inc., 3–32.

— 2000b. "The consumption of space and the spaces of consumption," in Mark Gottdiener, ed., *New Forms of Consumption: Consumers, Culture, and Commodification*. Lanham: Rowman and Littlefield Publishers, Inc., 265–86.

Gottschang, Suzanne K. 2000. "A baby-friendly hospital and the science of infant feeding," in Jun Jing, ed., *Feeding China's Little Emperors: Food, Children, and Social Change*. Stanford: Stanford University Press, 160–84.

Graff, Amy. 2013. "Chinese birth tourism booms in southern California," *SFGate*. (online) March 15, 2013. Available at http://blog.sfgate.com/sfmoms/2013/03/15/chinese-birth-tourism-booms-in-southern-california/ (accessed October 23, 2013).

Greenblatt, Alan. 2013. "What China's unique urbanization can teach America," *Governing*. Available at http://www.governing.com/topics/economic-dev/gov-what-chinas-unique-urbanization-can-teach-america.html (accessed October 23, 2013).

Greenhalgh, Susan. 2008. *Just One Child: Science and Policy in Deng's China*. Berkeley: University of California Press.

Grenoble, Ryan. 2013. "1000 dead ducks found in China's Nanhe River: Pig carcass count continues to rise," *The Huffington Post*. (online) March 26, 2013. Available at http://www.huffingtonpost.com/2013/03/26/dead-ducks-china-river_n_2951711.html#slide=2204520 (accessed October 23, 2013).

Griffiths, Michael B. 2013. *Consumers and Individuals in China: Standing Out, Fitting In*. New York: Routledge.

Habermas, Jürgen. 1989. *The Structural Transformation of the Public Sphere*. Trans. Thomas Burger. Cambridge: MIT Press.

Hall, Stuart. 2002. "Political belonging in a world of multiple identities," in Steven Vertovec and Robin Cohen, eds., *Conceiving Cosmopolitanism: Theory, Context, and Practice*. Oxford University Press, 25–31.

Hansegard, Jens. 2012. "IKEA taking China by storm." *Wall Street Journal*. (online) March 26, 2012. Available at http://online.wsj.com/article/SB1000 142405270230463640457729308348182153536.html (accessed December 23, 2013).

Hanser, Amy. 2008. *Service Encounters: Class, Gender, and the Market for Social Distinction in Urban China*. Stanford University Press.

Harvey, David. 1990. "Between space and time: Reflections on the geographical imagination," *Annals of the Association of American Geographers*, 80(3): 418–24.

Herold, David Kurt and Peter Marolt, eds. 2011. *Online Society in China: Creating, Celebrating, and Instrumentalising the Online Carnival*. New York: Routledge.

— 2011. "Conclusion: Netizens and citizens, cyberspace and modern China," in David Kurt Herold and Peter Marolt, eds., *Online Society in China: Creating, Celebrating, and Instrumentalising the Online Carnival*. New York: Routledge, 200–8.

Herz, Ellen. 2001. "Face in the crowd: The cultural construction of anonymity in urban China," in Nancy N. Chen, Constance D. Clark, Suzanne Z. Gottschang, and Lyn Jeffery, eds., *China Urban*. Duke University Press, 274–94.

Hine, Tomas. 2002. *I Want That: How We All Became Shoppers*. New York: HarperCollins.

Hjorth, Larissa and Michael Arnold. 2012. "Home and away: A case study of students and social media in Shanghai," in Pui-lam Law, ed., *New Connectivities in China: Virtual, Actual and Local Interactions*. New York: Springer, 171–84.

Honig, Emily and Gail Hershatter. 1988. *Personal Voices: Chinese Women in the 1980s*. Stanford University Press.

hooks, bell. 2000. "Eating the other: Desire and resistance," in Juliet B. Schor and Douglas B. Holt, eds., *The Consumer Society Reader*. New York: The New Press, 343–59.

Huffington Post. 2011. "McDonald's China plans to open a new store every day in four years." (online) July 29, 2011. Available at http://www.huffingtonpost .com/2011/07/29/mcdonalds-china-new-stores_n_913071.html (accessed October 23, 2013).

— 2012. "Starbucks China to be second largest market outside of US in 2014." (online) November 27, 2011. Available at http://www.huffingtonpost

.com/2012/11/27/starbucks-china_n_2197554.html (accessed October 23, 2013).

Jacobs, Andrew. 2013. "New leaders in China speak of reform, end to corruption," *New York Times*. (online) March 18, 2013. Available at http://www .bostonglobe.com/news/world/2013/03/17/new-chinese-leader-promises -government-reforms/ps4CsKRHHblTQ0Fm6KMazK/story.html (accessed December 23, 2013).

Jing, Jun. 2000. "Introduction: Food, children, and social change in contemporary China," in Jun Jing, ed., *Feeding China's Little Emperors: Food, Children, and Social Change*. Stanford University Press, 1–26.

Kane, Claire and Victoria Bryan. 2013. "Chinese overtake Germans as biggest spending tourists," *Reuters*. (online) April 4, 2013. Available at http://www .reuters.com/article/2013/04/04/us-china-tourism-spending-idUSBRE 9330TJ20130404 (accessed October 24, 2013).

Keane, Michael. 2006. "From made in China to created in China," *International Journal of Cultural Studies*, 9(3): 285–96.

Koch, P., et al. 2009. "Beauty is in the eye of the QQ User: Instant messaging in China," in G. Goggin and M. McLelland, eds., *Internationalizing Internet studies*. London: Routledge, 265–84.

Lefebvre, Henri. 1996. *Writings on Cities*. Ed. and trans. Eleonore Kofman and Elizabeth Lebas. Oxford: Blackwell.

Li, Cheng, ed. 2010. *China's Emerging Middle Class: Beyond Economic Transformation*. Washington D.C.: Brookings Institution Press.

Li, Jiabao. 2013. "Carrefour's China revenues grow 10.8%," *China Daily*. (online) January 23, 2013. Available at http://www.chinadaily.com.cn/bizchina/ 2013-01/23/content_16166626.htm (accessed October 23, 2013).

Li, Woke. 2013. "Shopping malls boom in China on urbanization." Chinadaily .com. At http://www.chinadaily.com.cn/bizchina/2013-01/10/content _16101869.htm (accessed October 23, 2013).

Liechty, Mark. 2003. *Suitably Modern: Making Middle-Class Culture in a New Consumer Society*. Princeton University Press.

Lin, Tien-wei. 2013. "China to have more than 4000 shopping malls by end of 2015," *Want China Times*. (online) January 9, 2013. Available at http://www .wantchinatimes.com/news-subclass-cnt.aspx?id=20130109000067&cid =1102 (accessed October 24, 2013).

Lin, Yi-Chieh Jessica. 2011. *Fake Stuff: China and the Rise of Counterfeit Goods*. Milton Park: Routledge.

Lozada, Eriberto P. 2000. "Globalized childhood: Kentucky fried chicken in Beijing," in Jun Jing, ed., *Feeding China's Little Emperors: Food, Children, and Social Change*. Stanford University Press, 114–34.

Lukacs, Gabriella. 2010. *Scripted Affects, Branded Selves*. Duke University Press.

McDonald, Mark. 2012. "From milk to peas, a Chinese food safety mess," *International New York Times*. (online) June 21, 2012. Available at http://rendezvous.blogs.nytimes.com/2012/06/21/from-milk-to-peas-a-chinese-food-safety-mess/?_r=0 (accessed October 24, 2013).

McGregor, James. 2005. *One Billion Customers: Lessons From the Front Lines of Doing Business in China*. New York: Wall Street Journal Books.

Maffesoli, Michel. 1996. *The Time of the Tribes: The Decline of Individualism in Mass Society*. London: Sage Publications.

Marolt, Peter. 2011. "Grassroots agency in a civil sphere? Rethinking Internet control in China," in David Kurt Herold and Peter Marolt, eds., *Online Society in China: Creating, Celebrating, and Instrumentalising the Online Carnival*. New York: Routledge, 53–68.

Marx, Karl. 1990. *Capital: A Critique of Political Economy*. London: Penguin Books.

Massey, Doreen. 2005. *For Space*. Thousand Oaks, CA: Sage Publications, Ltd.

Mauss, Marcel. 1990. *The Gift*. London: Routledge.

Meyer, Michael. 2008. *The Last Days of Old Beijing*. New York: Walker and Company.

Michael, David C. 2012. "China's digital generation 3.0: The online empire." *Boston Consulting Group Perspectives*. (online) April 11, 2012. Available at https://www.bcgperspectives.com/content/articles/digital_economy_globalization_china_digital_3_0_online_empire/ (accessed October 23, 2013).

Miller, Daniel. 1987. *Material Culture and Mass Consumption*. New York: Basil Blackwell Inc.

— 1998. *A Theory of Shopping*. Cornell University Press.

Miller, Daniel, Peter Jackson, Nigel Thrift, Beverley Holbrook and Michael Rowlands. 1998. *Shopping, Place and Identity*. New York: Routledge.

Millward, Steven. 2012. "China's forgotten 3rd Twitter clone hits 260 million users," *Tech In Asia*. (online) October 22, 2012. Available at http://www.techinasia.com/netease-weibo-260-million-users-numbers/ (accessed October 23, 2013).

Minemura, Kenji. 2010. "China bans reporting on 18 subjects," *The Asahi Shimbun*. (online) March 26, 2010. Available at http://www.asahi.com/english/TKY201003250329.html (accessed October 23, 2013).

Naughton, Barry. 1995. "Cities in the Chinese economic system: Changing roles and conditions for autonomy," in Deborah S. Davis, Richard Kraus, Barry Naughton and Elizabeth J. Perry, eds., *Urban Spaces in China*. New York: Cambridge University Press, 61–89.

Oh, Minjoo and Jorge Arditi. 2000."Shopping and postmodernism: Consumption, production, identity, and the internet," in Mark Gottdiener, ed., *New Forms of Consumption*. Lanham: Rowman and Littlefield Publishers, Inc., 71–92.

Ong, Aihwa. 1997."Chinese Modernities: Narratives of Nation and of Capitalism," in Aihwa Ong and Donald Nonini, eds., *Ungrounded Empires: The Cultural Politics of Modern Chinese Transnationalism*. New York: Routledge, 171–202.

— 1999. *Flexible Citizenship: The Cultural Logics of Transnationality*. Durham: Duke University Press.

Ong, Aihwa and Donald Nonini, eds. 1997. *Ungrounded Empires: The Cultural Politics of Modern Chinese Transnationalism*. New York: Routledge.

Otis, Eileen. 2012. *Markets and Bodies: Women, Service Work, and the Making of Inequality in China*. Stanford University Press.

People's Daily Online. 2008."The number of cities in China reached 655." (online) November 5, 2008. Available at http://english.people.com.cn/90001/90776/90882/6528090.html (accessed October 24, 2013).

— 2011."China expects urbanization rate to be 51.5% by 2015." (online) March 5, 2011. Available at http://english.people.com.cn/90001/90776/90785/7309349.html (accessed October 24, 2013).

Pierson, David. 2011. "In China, fake phones are losing appeal," *Los Angeles Times*. (online) October 4, 2011. Available at http://articles.latimes.com/2011/oct/04/business/la-fi-china-fake-phones-20111004 (accessed October 23, 2013).

Qiang, Xiao. 2011."The rise of online public opinion and its political impact," in Susan Shirk, ed., *Changing Media, Changing China*. Oxford University Press, 202–24.

Ren, Xuefei. 2013. *Urban China*. Cambridge: Polity.

Reporters Without Borders. "Freedom of the press worldwide in 2013." Available at http://en.rsf.org/press-freedom-index-2013,1054.html (accessed October 23, 2013).

Ritzer, George. 2010. *Enchanting a Disenchanted World: Continuity and change in the cathedrals of consumption*. Thousand Oaks, CA: Pine Forge Press.

Ritzer, George and Seth Ovadia. 2000. "The process of McDonaldization is not uniform, nor are its settings, consumers, or the consumption of its goods and services," in Mark Gottdiener, ed., *New Forms of Consumption: Consumers, Culture, and Commodification*. Lanham: Rowman and Littlefield Publishers, Inc., 33–50.

Rofel, Lisa. 1999. *Other Modernities: Gendered Yearnings in China After Socialism*. Berkeley: University of California Press.

— 2007. *Desiring China: Experiments in Neoliberalism, Sexuality, and Public Culture*. Duke University Press.

Rojek, Chris. 2000. "Mass tourism or the re-enchantment of the world? Issues and contradictions in the study of travel," in Mark Gottdiener, ed., *New Forms of Consumption: Consumers, Culture, and Commodification*. Lanham: Rowman and Littlefield Publishers, Inc., 51–70.

Sassan, Saskia. 1991. *The Global City: New York, London, Tokyo*. Princeton University Press.

Schein, Louisa. 2000. *Minority rules: the Miao and the feminine in China's cultural politics*. Durham: Duke University Press.

— 2001. "Urbanity, cosmopolitanism, consumption," in Nancy N. Chen, Constance D. Clark, Suzanne Z. Gottschang, and Lyn Jeffery, eds., *China Urban*. Duke University Press, 225–41.

Schor, Juliet B. 2000. "Towards a new politics of consumption," in Juliet B. Schor and Douglas B. Holt, eds., *The Consumer Society Reader*. New York: The New Press, 446–62.

Schor, Juliet B. and Douglas B. Holt, eds. 2000. *The Consumer Society Reader*. New York: The New Press.

Sensenbrenner, Julia S. 2000. "Commercializing childhood: Parental purchases for Shanghai's only child," in Deborah S. Davis, ed., *The Consumer Revolution in Urban China*. Berkeley: University of California Press, 54–79.

Shapiro, Judith. 2012. *China's Environmental Challenges*. Malden, MA: Polity.

Shields, Rob. 1992. *Lifestyle Shopping: The Subject of Consumption*. New York: Routledge.

Shirk, Susan, ed. 2011. *Changing Media, Changing China*. New York: Oxford University Press.

Silverstein, Michael. 2012. "Don't underestimate China's luxury market," *Harvard Business Review*. (online) December 12, 2012. Available at http://blogs.hbr .org/2012/12/chinas-luxury-market-and/ (accessed October 23, 2012).

Simmel, Georg. 1950. *The Sociology of Georg Simmel*. Compiled and translated by Kurt Wolff. Glencoe, IL: Free Press.

Slater, Don. 1997. *Consumer Culture and Modernity*. Cambridge: Polity.

Stout, Kristie Lu. 2013. "Can social media clear air over China?" in *CNN*. (online) April 19, 2013. Available at http://www.cnn.com/2013/04/19/world/asia/ lu-stout-china-pollution/ (accessed October 23, 2013).

Sugiyama, Satomi. 2009. "Decorated mobile phones and emotional attachment for Japanese youths" in Jane Vincent and Leopoldina Fortunati, eds., *Electronic Emotion: The mediation of emotion via information and communication technologies*. Bern: Peter Lang AG, International Academic Publishers, 85–105.

Thompson, Derek. 2012. "The world's fastest growing and fastest shrinking cities in 2012," *The Atlantic*. (online) November 30, 2012. Available at http://www.theatlantic.com/business/archive/2012/11/the-worlds-fastest-growing-and-fastest-shrinking-cities-in-2012/265781/ (accessed October 24, 2013).

Trentmann, Frank. 2006. "The evolution of the consumer: Meanings, identities, and political synapses before the age of affluence," in Sheldon Garon and Patricia L. Maclachlan, eds., *The Ambivalent Consumer: Questioning Consumption in East Asia and the West*. Ithaca: Cornell University Press, 21–44.

Twitchell, James. 2000. "Two cheers for materialism," in Juliet B. Schor and Douglas B. Holt, eds., *The Consumer Society Reader*. New York: The New Press, 281–90.

Veblen, Thorstein. 1899. *The Theory of the Leisure Class: An Economic Study of Institutions*. New York: Macmillan Company.

Volland, Nicolai. 2011. "Taking urban conservation online: Chinese civic action groups and the Internet," in David Kurt Herold and Peter Marolt, eds., *Online Society in China: Creating, Celebrating, and Instrumentalising the Online Carnival*. New York: Routledge, 184–99.

Wall, Kim. 2013. "IKEA at last cracks China market," *South China Morning Post*. (online) September 1, 2013. Available at http://www.scmp.com/news/china/article/1300942/ikea-last-cracks-china-market-success-has-meant-adapting-local-ways?page=all (accessed October 24, 2013).

Wang, Jing. 2008. *Brand New China*. Cambridge: Harvard University Press.

Wang, Shaoguang. 1995. "The politics of private time: Changing leisure patterns in urban China," in Deborah S. Davis, Richard Kraus, Barry Naughton and Elizabeth J. Perry, eds., *Urban Spaces in China*. New York: Cambridge University Press, 149–72.

Want China Times. 2012. "China luxury goods buyers 25 years younger than counterparts." (online) Available at http://www.wantchinatimes.com/news-subclass-cnt.aspx?id=20120816000046&cid=1102 (accessed October 23, 2013).

Wasserstrom, Jeffrey. 2009. "Middle-class mobilization," *Journal of Democracy*, 20(3): 29–32.

Wasserstrom, Jeffrey N. and Liu Xinyong. 1995. "Student associations and mass movements," in Deborah S. Davis, Richard Kraus, Barry Naughton, and Elizabeth J. Perry, eds., *Urban Spaces in China*. New York: Cambridge University Press, 362–93.

Watson, James L. 2000. "Food as a lens: The past, present, and future of family life in China," in Jun Jing, ed., *Feeding China's Little Emperors: Food, Children, and Social Change*. Stanford University Press, 199–212.

Weber, Max. 2005. *Economy and Society*. Stanford University Press.

Wohlsen, Marcus. 2012. "WalMart's master plan to sell itself to China," August 16, 2012, *Wired*, at http://www.wired.com/business/2012/08/walmarts-master-plan-to-sell-china-to-itself/ (accessed October 23, 2013).

Wong, Edward. 2013. "As pollution worsens in China, solutions succumb to infighting," *The New York Times*. (online) March 21, 2013. Available at http://www.nytimes.com/2013/03/22/world/asia/as-chinas-environmental-woes-worsen-infighting-emerges-as-biggest-obstacle.html (accessed October 23, 2013).

Wu, Fulong. 2010. "Gated and packaged suburbia: Packaging and branding Chinese suburban residential development," *Cities*, 27(5): 385–96.

Yan, Yunxiang. 1997. "McDonald's in Beijing: The localization of Americana," in James L. Watson, ed., *Golden Arches East: McDonald's in East Asia*. Stanford University Press, 39–76.

— 2000. "Of hamburger and social space: Consuming McDonald's in Beijing," in Deborah S. Davis, ed., *The Consumer Revolution in Urban China*. Berkeley: University of California Press, 201–25.

— 2003. *Private Life Under Socialism: Love, Intimacy, and Family Change in a Chinese Village 1949–1999*. Stanford University Press.

Yang, Mayfair Mei-Hui. 1994. *Gifts, Favors, and Banquets: The Art of Social Relationships in China*. Cornell University Press.

— 1997. "Mass media and transnational subjectivity in Shanghai: Notes on (re)cosmopolitanism in a Chinese metropolis," in Aihwa Ong and Donald Nonini, eds., *Ungrounded Empires: The Cultural Politics of Modern Chinese Transnationalism*. New York: Routledge, 287–322.

Yu, LiAnne and Tai Hou Tng. 2003. "Culture and design for mobile phones in China," in James E. Katz, ed., *Machines That Become Us: The Social Context of Personal Communication Technology*. New Brunswick: Transaction Publishers.

Zhang, Li. 2010. *In Search of Paradise: Middle Class Living in a Chinese Metropolis*. Ithaca, NY: Cornell University Press.

Zukin, Sharon. 2004. *Point of Purchase: How Shopping Changed American Culture*. New York: Routledge.

Index